Weight equivalents

METRIC	IMPERIAL	METRIC	IMPERIAL
10g	$^1/_4$oz	400g	14oz
15g	$^1/_2$oz	450g	1lb
20g	$^3/_4$oz	500g	1lb 2oz
25g	scant 1oz	550g	$1^1/_4$lb
30g	1oz	600g	1lb 5oz
45g	$1^1/_2$oz	675g	$1^1/_2$lb
50g	$1^3/_4$oz	750g	1lb 10oz
60g	2oz	800g	$1^3/_4$lb
75g	$2^1/_2$oz	900g	2lb
85g	3oz	1kg	$2^1/_4$lb
100g	$3^1/_2$oz	1.1kg	$2^1/_2$lb
115g	4oz	1.25kg	$2^3/_4$lb
125g	$4^1/_2$oz	1.35kg	3lb
140g	5oz	1.5kg	3lb 3oz
150g	$5^1/_2$oz	1.8kg	4lb
175g	6oz	2kg	$4^1/_2$lb
200g	7oz	2.25kg	5lb
250g	9oz	2.5kg	$5^1/_2$lb
300g	10oz	2.7kg	6lb
350g	12oz	3kg	$6^1/_2$lb

everyday easy

Cakes
& cupcakes

cheesecakes • traybakes
light sponges • creamy gâteaux

LONDON, NEW YORK, MELBOURNE,
MUNICH, AND DELHI

Editor Shashwati Tia Sarkar
Project Art Editors Elly King, Kathryn Wilding
Senior Jackets Creative Nicola Powling
Managing Editor Dawn Henderson
Managing Art Editor Marianne Markham
Senior Production Editor Jennifer Murray
Production Controller Poppy Newdick

DK INDIA

Editorial Manager Glenda Fernandes
Designer Neha Ahuja
Editor Alicia Ingty
Assistant Designer Nidhi Mehra
Assistant Editor Megha Gupta
DTP Co-ordinator Sunil Sharma
DTP Operator Saurabh Challariya

Material first published in *The Cooking Book* (2008), *Cook Express* (2009), and *The Fairtrade Everyday Cookbook* (2008)

This edition first published in Great Britain in 2010
by Dorling Kindersley Limited
80 Strand, London WC2R 0RL

A Penguin Company

Copyright © 2008, 2009, 2010 Dorling Kindersley
Text copyright © 2008, 2009, 2010 Dorling Kindersley

2 4 6 8 10 9 7 5 3 1

007 - CD266 - Oct/10

ISBN 978-1-4053-5646-6

Printed and bound in China by Leo

Discover more at
www.dk.com

CONTENTS

USEFUL INFORMATION 6
TECHNIQUES 8
RECIPE CHOOSERS 20

SPONGE CAKES 30

FRUITY CAKES 62

LOAF CAKES 94

TRAYBAKES & SLICES 112

SMALL BAKES & MUFFINS 144

CUPCAKES 166

CHEESECAKES 190

MERINGUE CAKES 208

INDEX 222
ACKNOWLEDGMENTS 224

Baking ingredients

Understanding your ingredients and how to use them will improve your baking. Always measure carefully and never mix metric and imperial measurements.

INGREDIENT	CHOOSE	USE
BUTTER	**BUTTER** Both **salted** or **unsalted butter** can be used for baking. Unsalted butter is mostly preferred in this book, but it's all down to taste preference, and whether you are reducing the salt in your diet. The amount of salt in salted butter varies, so check the label. Salted butter will keep for longer if you keep it in a butter dish out of the refrigerator.	Salted or unsalted, for cakes and bakes. Use softened butter (at room temperature). This means plenty of air will be held by the fat as you mix, making your cake or bake lighter.
SUGAR	**SUGAR** **Caster sugar** is finer than **granulated**. Use unrefined sugar (golden caster sugar) if you can. It is more natural than **white refined sugar**, which is processed and stripped of its molasses. **Unrefined sugar** adds a slight caramel flavour to your baking. **"Brown" sugar** is also white refined sugar, but it has the molasses added back to it.	Caster sugar, unrefined if possible, for cakes and bakes. White and brown sugars are equally sweet but the molasses in brown sugar create a moister texture.
BAKING POWDER	**BAKING POWDER** This is a raising agent used in baking. It is a mixture of bicarbonate of soda and cream of tartar, a natural raising agent, and is different to **baking soda or bicarbonate of soda**, as it doesn't contain cream of tartar. The two cannot be interchanged. Check the sell-by date of baking powder, as its effect wears off when it's old.	Cakes and biscuits. If a recipe calls for self-raising flour and you haven't got any, add baking powder to plain flour (4 tsp per 225g (8oz).
FLOUR	**FLOUR** **Plain flour** and **self-raising flour** are quite low in gluten, unlike strong bread flour. There are many flours that are suitable for a wheat-free or gluten-free diet, such as **rice flour**, **chestnut flour**, and **potato flour**. If using, consult specialist recipes as they are not interchangeable with plain flour.	Plain flour or self-raising flour, sifted, for cakes and bakes. Don't over-beat once flour has been added, as the gluten will strengthen and you'll get a tough texture. This is why flour is folded in.
EGGS	**EGGS** Choose **organic** and/or **free-range hens'** eggs, as they will improve the flavour and quality of your finished cake.	Use at room temperature. If they are used cold from the refrigerator, they cool the butter down and the mixture can curdle.

Tools of the trade

Cake tins should be rigid and sturdy, so they don't buckle in the heat of the oven. A selection of sizes and shapes is useful. For making a 4-egg sponge cake, you will need two 20cm (8in) sandwich tins. Loose-bottomed cake tins are great – they make turning the cake out a lot easier. A springform cake tin is useful for larger cakes, or more fragile ones such as a baked cheesecake.

If you are switching your pans from square to round, go up 2.5cm (1in) in size. If your recipe calls for a round 18cm (7in) pan, you can use an 20cm (8in) square pan. If switching the other way, from round to square, go down 2.5cm (1in).

Baking sheets should be rigid and sturdy, so they don't buckle in the heat. Have a selection with and without lips.

A wire rack is necessary for cooling all cakes and bakes. Choose a large one if you plan to do batch baking.

Paper cases are available in a variety of sizes but the main categories are standard cupcake or fairy cases, muffin cases, and mini muffin cases. Heed the recipe when it specifies a paper case size – the wrong size will give you a different yield.

A small collection of essential baking tools is all you need to start baking.

A guide to symbols

The recipes in this book are accompanied by symbols that alert you to important information.

 Tells you how many people the recipe serves, or how much is produced.

 Indicates how much time you will need to prepare and cook a dish. Next to this symbol you will also find out if additional time is required for such things as chilling, soaking, or proving. Read the recipe to find out exactly how much extra time to allow.

 This is especially important, as it alerts you to what has to be done before you can begin to cook the recipe, or to parts of the recipe that may take a long time to complete.

 This denotes that special equipment is required, such as a springform tin or special mould. Where possible, alternatives are given.

 This symbol accompanies freezing information.

TECHNIQUES

Test eggs for freshness

As well as the best-before date on the egg box, you can use this simple test to check how fresh your eggs are: immerse the egg in water and see if it rises. A stale egg contains much more air and less liquid than a fresh one, so it will float. Do not use a stale egg.

Fresh   Borderline   Stale

Separate eggs

Many recipes call for either yolks or whites. Smell the eggs first to be sure they are fresh, or use the floating test above.

1 Break the shell of a cold egg by tapping it against the rim of a bowl. Insert your fingers into the break and gently pry the two halves apart.

2 Gently shift the yolk back and forth between the shell halves, allowing the white to separate and fall into the bowl. Take care to keep the yolk intact.

Whisk egg whites

For the best results, use a clean, dry glass or metal bowl and a balloon whisk. The whites must be completely free of yolk, or any other contact with grease.

1 Place the egg whites in the bowl (here a copper bowl is used) and begin whisking slowly, using a small range of motion.

2 Continue whisking steadily, using larger strokes, until the whites have lost their translucency and start to foam.

3 Incorporating as much air as possible, increase your speed and range of motion until the whites peak to the desired degree and are stiff but not dry.

4 Test by lifting the whisk; the peaks should be firm but glossy and the tips should hang.

Make sponge cake

This method will produce a light, buttery sponge. Use two 20cm (8in) sandwich tins to make 2 sponges, which you can fill with fruit or cream if you like.

1 Preheat the oven to 180°C (350°F/Gas 4). In a bowl, cream together 225g (8oz) softened butter and 225g (8oz) caster sugar with an electric mixer or wooden spoon until pale and fluffy.

2 Lightly beat 4 room-temperature eggs. Add little by little to the butter and sugar, beating well. Add 1 tbsp of sifted flour, taken from 225g (8oz) self-raising flour, to prevent it from curdling.

3 Once all the egg is added, use a metal spoon to fold in the rest of the flour. The mixture should drop off the spoon easily when it is ready. Add 1 tbsp of water if the mixture is too thick.

4 Divide the mixture between 2 tins, and smooth out. Bake for 20 minutes, or until the cakes have risen, are golden, and feel springy to the touch. Allow to cool slightly in the tins before turning out.

Prepare and line a cake tin

Greasing then flouring or lining your tin ensures that baked layers turn out cleanly and easily.

1 Melt unsalted butter (unless your recipe states otherwise) and use a pastry brush to apply a thin, even layer over the bottom and sides of the tin, making sure to brush butter into the corners.

2 Then, sprinkle a small amount of flour into the tin. Shake the pan so the flour coats the bottom and rotate the tin to coat the sides. Turn the tin upside down and tap to remove the excess flour.

3 Or, to line with baking parchment instead of flour, stand the tin on the paper and draw around the base with a pencil. Cut out the shape just inside the pencil line.

4 Place the piece of baking parchment directly on to the greased bottom of the cake tin. It should fit neatly inside and into the corners. This layer can be peeled off once your cake is cooked and cooled.

Make cheesecake

This simple basic recipe for a no-cook chilled cheesecake can be adapted by adding your own fruit and flavours. It makes an 8in (20cm) cheesecake.

1 Process 250g (9oz) of digestive biscuits in a food processor until crumbled, or place in a plastic bag and crush with a rolling pin. Melt 140g (5oz) of butter and stir in the biscuit crumbs. Spoon into a loose-bottomed flan tin, and spread evenly.

2 Put 3 tsp of powdered gelatine into a glass bowl with the juice of 3–4 lemons. Stir in 1 tsp of water, and sit the bowl over a pan of simmering water. Stir until the gelatine dissolves. Add 50g (1³/₄oz) of caster sugar, and continue stirring until it dissolves.

3 Make the topping by lightly whisking 400ml (14fl oz) of double cream, then adding 225g (8oz) of mascarpone, and 250g (9oz) of cream cheese. Add a couple of drops of vanilla extract, then pour in the gelatine mixture. Stir well to combine.

4 Pour the mixture over the base, and smooth the top. To set, put in the refrigerator for about 2 hours, or overnight. Make sure it is completely set before releasing it from the tin. Dust with icing sugar and decorate with berries to serve.

Roll a sponge roulade

A roulade is less likely to tear if filled and rolled while it is still warm and flexible. Take care not to over-fill before rolling it, too.

1 Carefully line a Swiss roll tin with a fitted piece of baking parchment. Make the mixture for the sponge cake, taking care to fold in the egg white mixture very gently with a metal spoon so that none of the volume is lost.

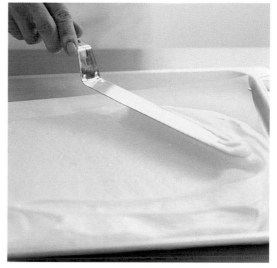

2 Spread the batter evenly in the Swiss roll tin using a spatula. Bake until golden and springy to the touch. Sprinkle with caster sugar and place a clean piece of baking parchment on top. Carefully turn the cake out face down on to a work surface.

3 Slowly peel away the top (old) layer of baking parchment, taking care not to tear the cake. Spread with your desired filling and roll up the cake, using the new piece of parchment to support the roulade with a little gentle pressure.

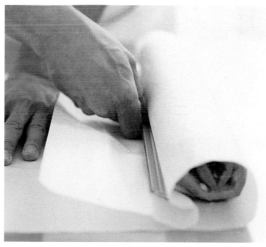

4 Fold one half of the parchment over the roulade. With the roulade in the centre, hold the bottom half and push a ruler against the roll with your free hand. This will tighten and shape the roulade evenly. Remove the paper, and trim the ends to serve.

Whip cream

You can whip cream to soft or stiff peaks. Chill the cream beforehand and put the cream in a bowl set over a large bowl of ice before whipping.

1 Start whipping slowly with about 2 strokes per second (or the lowest speed on an electric mixer) until the cream begins to thicken.

2 Increase to a moderate speed for soft peaks. For stiff peaks, continue beating and test by lifting the beaters to see if the cream retains its shape.

Pipe

A piping bag can be used to pipe not only whipped cream, but also buttercream icing, meringue, and choux pastry.

1 Place the nozzle in the bag and twist to seal. Hold the bag just above the nozzle, fold the top of the bag over to create a "collar", and spoon in the filling. Continue until the bag is ³/₄ full.

2 Twist the top of the bag to close and expel any air. Holding the twisted end taut in one hand, use your other hand to gently press the filling to start a steady flow and direct the nozzle as desired.

Prepare chocolate

Chill the chocolate before cutting and grating, as the warmth of your hands will quickly melt it.

For chopping, break the chocolate into small pieces, then chill the pieces in the freezer for a few minutes. Place on a cutting board and use a sharp knife to chop using a rocking motion.

For grating, rub chilled chocolate against the face of the grater, using the widest holes. If the chocolate begins to melt, chill it again in the freezer and continue grating once it has hardened.

To melt chocolate, gently simmer some water in a pan. Place chopped chocolate in a heatproof bowl and set it over the water. Let the chocolate melt, then it stir with a wooden spoon until smooth.

For curls, spread soft or melted chocolate on to a cool marble surface. Use the blade of a large knife to scrape the chocolate into curls.

17

Rich vanilla buttercream icing

This simple recipe can be used to ice cupcakes and sandwich cake layers together. You could add a few drops of food colouring, if you wish.

INGREDIENTS

115g (4oz) unsalted butter, at room temperature
2 tbsp milk
1 tsp pure vanilla extract
225g (8oz) icing sugar

METHOD

1 Put the butter, half the milk, and the vanilla extract in a large mixing bowl and beat until smooth and blended using an electric hand whisk.

2 Sift over the icing sugar and, with the whisk on a low speed, continue mixing until the icing is smooth and has a spreading consistency. If it is too stiff, beat in a little extra milk.

PREPARE AHEAD The icing will keep, covered, in the refrigerator for 2 days. If it is too stiff to spread, stir in a little extra milk.

makes 350g (12oz)

prep 10 mins

electric hand whisk

Crème pâtissière

This sweet pastry cream is great for European-style cakes and desserts.

INGREDIENTS
300ml (10fl oz) milk
2 egg yolks
60g (2oz) caster sugar
20g ($^3/_4$oz) plain flour
20g ($^3/_4$oz) cornflour
$^1/_4$ tsp pure vanilla extract

METHOD
1 Pour the milk into a saucepan and heat it to simmering point.

2 Beat the eggs and sugar together in a bowl, mix in the flour and cornflour, then pour in the hot milk, and mix well.

3 Return the mixture to the pan and bring it slowly to the boil, stirring continuously until it becomes smooth and lump-free. Once the mixture reaches boiling point, reduce the heat, and simmer, stirring for 1–2 minutes, to cook the flour.

4 Allow it to cool a little, then stir in the vanilla extract. Use at once, or cover and chill until needed.

PREPARE AHEAD The crème pâtissière can be made 1 day in advance, covered with cling film, and chilled in a refrigerator until ready to use.

makes 300ml
(10fl oz)

prep 10 mins
• cook 5 mins

Celebration

Blueberry and pistachio angel cupcakes page 184

Chocolate cake with chocolate fudge icing page 46

Toffee-topped banana cake page 90

Black Forest gâteaux page 92

Bienenstich page 44

Orange and lemon cupcakes page 172

Tropical angel cake page 84

Celebration cake page 86

Vanilla cupcakes page 168

Chocolate log page 48

Coconut and lime cake
page 80

Sachertorte page 52

21

Great for kids

Strawberry and cream cupcakes page 182

Chocolate biscuit cake page 142

Apple muffins page 160

Sticky toffee shortbreads page 124

Fondant fancies page 152

Madeleines page 146

White chocolate and macadamia nut blondies page 116

Orange and lemon cupcakes page 172

Banana and chocolate chip muffins page 158

Sticky date flapjacks page 122

Chocolate-frosted cupcakes page 170

Cherry and coconut cupcakes page 186

Mini banana and chocolate cheesecakes page 206

Chocolate and buttercream Swiss roll page 42

Quick

Nutty "drop" buns page 150

Swiss roll page 40

Chocolate muffins page 164

Chocolate biscuit cake page 142

Lemon poppy seed muffins page 156

Carrot cake page 76

Madeleines page 146

Blueberry muffins page 162

Strawberry cheesecake page 194

French almond financiers
page 148

Black cherry cheesecake page 202

With tea

Light fruitcake page 64

Lemon, lime, and poppy seed cake page 100

Tropical fruit and ginger cake page 72

Marble cake page 54

Apricot crumble shortbread page 134

Berry friands page 154

Banana, cranberry, and walnut loaf page 104

Orange and pistachio cake page 74

Marmalade and ginger loaf
page 106

Lime drizzle cupcakes page 180

Sticky lemon cake page 68

Superfood loaf cake page 108

Victoria sponge cake page 38

After dinner

Mocha slices page 126

Toffee apple traybake
page 138

White chocolate cakes
page 140

Meringue and rum layer cake
page 216

Apple streusel cake page 82

Pear and chocolate cake page 88

Honey cake page 58

Classic Pavlova page 214

Chocolate Amaretti roulade
page 50

Baked stem ginger cheesecake
page 200

Blueberry-ripple cheesecake
page 198

Mountain meringue cake
page 220

Black cherry cheesecake
page 202

Rhubarb and ginger meringue cake page 218

Madeira cake

A traditional moist cake with a close texture and a hint of lemon.

INGREDIENTS

150g (5^1/$_2$oz) unsalted butter, at room temperature
150g (5^1/$_2$oz) caster sugar
3 eggs, lightly beaten
225g (8oz) self-raising flour
juice of 1 lemon

METHOD

1 Preheat the oven to 180°C (350°F/Gas 4). Put the butter and sugar in a mixing bowl and beat with an electric hand whisk or a wooden spoon until pale and creamy.

2 Beating all the time, add the eggs a little at a time, along with a little of the flour to stop the mixture curdling. Stir in the lemon juice, then fold in the rest of the flour with a metal spoon. Spoon the mixture into the lightly greased cake tin.

3 Bake for 1–1^1/$_2$ hours, or until cooked through. To test, pierce the centre of the cake with a skewer – if it comes out clean, the cake is cooked. Remove from the oven and leave to cool for 10 minutes in the tin, then run a knife around the edge to loosen. Leave to cool completely, then turn out on to a plate and serve.

serves 4–6

prep 15 mins
• cook
1–1^1/$_2$ hrs

18cm (7in)
round cake tin

freeze for
up to 3 months

Vanilla sponge cake

This light, butter-free sponge goes well with a number of fillings. This version uses buttercream and lemon curd for a zingy tartness to balance the vanilla.

INGREDIENTS

2 eggs, lightly beaten
75g (2$\frac{1}{2}$oz) caster sugar
a few drops of pure vanilla extract
75g (2$\frac{1}{2}$oz) self-raising flour
50g (1$\frac{3}{4}$oz) unsalted butter, at room temperature
125g (4$\frac{1}{2}$oz) icing sugar, plus extra for dusting
2 tbsp lemon curd

METHOD

1 Preheat the oven to 180°C (350°F/Gas 4). Put the eggs and sugar in a mixing bowl, and whisk with a balloon whisk or an electric hand whisk or until pale and creamy. Add a few drops of the vanilla extract.

2 Sift in the flour, a little at a time, folding each batch in gently with a metal spoon before adding more. Pour the mixture into the lightly greased cake tin. Bake in the oven for 30 minutes, or until lightly golden. To test, pierce the centre of the cake with a skewer – if it comes out clean, the cake is cooked. Remove from the oven, and leave to cool in the tin for 10–15 minutes, then loosen the edges with a knife and leave to cool completely.

3 Meanwhile, put the butter in a mixing bowl and beat with a wooden spoon for a few minutes until creamy. Sift in the icing sugar, beat well, then add a few drops of vanilla extract and beat again. Remove the cake from the tin and slice in half horizontally. Cover the bottom half with the buttercream and the top half with the lemon curd. Sandwich together, dust with icing sugar, and serve.

serves 4–6

prep 15 mins
• cook 30 mins

18cm (7in)
round cake tin

freeze, before
filling, for up to
3 months

Angel food cake

This American cake made with egg whites has a light texture that is similar to soft meringue.

INGREDIENTS

150g (5$\frac{1}{2}$oz) plain flour
100g (3$\frac{1}{2}$oz) icing sugar
8 egg whites
pinch of cream of tartar
250g (9oz) caster sugar
few drops of pure almond extract or pure vanilla extract
fresh mixed berries, to serve

For the frosting

150g (5$\frac{1}{2}$oz) caster sugar
1 egg white

METHOD

1 Preheat the oven to 180°C (350°F/Gas 4). Sift the flour and icing sugar together into a bowl.

2 In a large clean, dry glass or metal bowl, whisk the egg whites and cream of tartar with a balloon whisk or an electric hand whisk until stiff, then whisk in the caster sugar, 1 tbsp at a time. Gradually sift the flour mixture over, folding it in with a metal spoon. Fold in the almond extract or vanilla extract.

3 Spoon the mixture gently into the lightly greased ring mould and level the surface. Place the mould on a baking tray and bake for 35–45 minutes, or until just firm to the touch.

4 Remove the cake from the oven, and invert the mould on to a wire rack. Leave the cake to cool, then ease out of the mould.

5 To make the frosting, place the caster sugar in a saucepan with 4 tbsp of water. Heat gently, stirring, until the sugar dissolves. Boil until the syrup reaches soft-boil stage (114–118°C/238–245°F), or until a little of the syrup forms a soft ball when dropped into very cold water.

6 Meanwhile, whisk the egg white with a clean balloon whisk or electric hand whisk with clean beaters until stiff. As soon as the sugar syrup reaches temperature, plunge the base of the pan into cold water to stop the syrup getting any hotter, then pour slowly on to the egg whites, while still whisking, until the frosting holds a stiff peak.

7 Working quickly, because the surface will set quite quickly, spread the frosting over the cake with a palette knife, swirling the surface to give it texture.

GOOD WITH Fresh mixed berries.

serves 8–12

**prep 30 mins
• cook 35–45 mins**

1.7 litre (3-pint) savarin ring mould • sugar thermometer

Victoria sponge cake

This English classic is a favourite that has stood the test of time.

INGREDIENTS

175g (6oz) unsalted butter, at room temperature
175g (6oz) caster sugar
3 eggs, lightly beaten
175g (6oz) self-raising flour
6–8 tbsp raspberry jam
150ml (5fl oz) double cream
icing sugar, to dust

METHOD

1 Preheat the oven to 190°C (375°F/Gas 5). Lightly grease and line the bottom of the tins with baking parchment.

2 Beat the butter and sugar together with a wooden spoon or electric hand whisk until pale and fluffy. It is important to beat the mixture well at this stage to incorporate as much air as possible, which helps prevent the eggs from curdling

3 Add the eggs a little at a time, beating well after each addition. If the mixture begins to curdle, beat in 1–2 tbsp of the flour. Sift the flour, and fold into the egg mixture using a large metal spoon or a spatula.

4 Divide the mixture equally between the prepared tins, and spread evenly to level the tops. Bake for 20–25 minutes, until pale golden and springy to the touch. Allow the cakes to cool in the tins for 5 minutes, before turning out on to a wire rack. Peel off the baking parchment, and allow to cool completely.

5 When the cakes are cool, place one upside down on a serving plate, and spread with the raspberry jam. Lightly whip the cream, until just holding its shape, and spread over the jam. Top with the remaining cake, and dust lightly with icing sugar before serving.

serves 8

prep 20 mins
• cook 20–25 mins

for best results, have all your ingredients at room temperature

two 20cm (8in) round sandwich tins

freeze for up to 1 month

Swiss roll

For best results, avoid over-filling the sponge, to prevent spillage, and roll it while it is still slightly warm.

INGREDIENTS

3 large eggs
100g (3¹/₂oz) caster sugar, plus extra to sprinkle
salt
75g (2¹/₂oz) self-raising flour
1 tsp pure vanilla extract
6 tbsp strawberry jam, raspberry jam, lemon curd,
   or hazelnut spread

METHOD

1 Preheat the oven to 200°C (400°F/Gas 6). Line the base and sides of the Swiss roll tin with baking parchment. In a large bowl set over a pan of simmering water, whisk the eggs, sugar, and a pinch of salt vigorously with a balloon whisk or with an electric hand whisk for 5 minutes, or until very thick and creamy – any of the mixture dripping from the beaters should sit on the surface for a few moments before sinking in.

2 Remove the bowl from the pan and sit it on a work surface. Whisk the mixture for another minute or two, until cool. Sift in the flour, add the vanilla extract, and fold in very gently with a metal spoon. Pour into the tin and gently level into the corners. Bake for 12–15 minutes, or until firm to the touch and the cake has shrunk away from the sides of the tin.

3 Sprinkle a large sheet of baking parchment with caster sugar, then turn the cake out face down on to it. Leave to cool for 5 minutes, then peel off the parchment the cake was cooked on. If the jam is too thick to spread, warm it in a pan, then spread it over the top of the cake. Make a small indent with the back of a knife along one of the short sides, about 2cm (³/₄in) in from the edge. With this side facing towards you, start to roll the cake up, using the parchment to keep it tightly rolled and in shape (see step-by-step technique on page 15). When the cake is completely rolled up, leave to cool in the parchment. Peel off the parchment and place the cake, joint downwards, on a serving plate. Dust with extra caster sugar, if needed, before serving.

serves 8–10

prep 20 mins
• cook 15 mins

32.5 x 23cm
(13 x 9in)
Swiss roll tin

Chocolate and buttercream Swiss roll

This classic is always a hit at children's parties.

INGREDIENTS

3 large eggs
75g (2$\frac{1}{2}$oz) caster sugar
50g (1$\frac{3}{4}$oz) plain flour
25g (scant 1oz) cocoa powder, plus extra to dust
75g (2$\frac{1}{2}$oz) butter, softened
125g (4$\frac{1}{2}$oz) icing sugar

METHOD

1 Preheat the oven to 200°C (400°F/Gas 6). Sit a large heatproof bowl over a pan of simmering water, add the eggs and sugar, and whisk vigorously with a balloon whisk or with an electric hand whisk for 5–10 minutes, or until the mixture is thick and creamy – any of the mixture dripping from the beaters should sit on the surface for a few moments before sinking in. Remove from the heat, then sift in the flour and cocoa powder, and fold in gently with a metal spoon.

2 Line the Swiss roll tin with baking parchment, then pour the mixture into the tin and level the top. Bake for 10 minutes, or until the sponge is springy to the touch. Remove from the oven, cover with a damp tea towel, and leave to cool.

3 Turn the sponge out face down on to a sheet of baking parchment dusted with cocoa powder. Peel off the parchment the cake was cooked on. Put the butter in a mixing bowl and beat with an electric hand whisk or wooden spoon until creamy. Beat in the icing sugar a little at a time, then spread the mixture over the top of the sponge. Using the parchment to help you, roll the sponge up, starting from one of the short sides (see step-by-step technique on page 15). Dust with more cocoa powder, if needed, and serve.

serves 8

**prep 25 mins
• cook 10 mins**

**20 x 30cm
(8 x 12in)
Swiss roll tin**

Bienenstich

This German recipe is also known as Bee Sting Cake.

INGREDIENTS

140g (5oz) plain flour
15g (¹/₂oz) unsalted butter, at
   room temperature
¹/₂ tbsp caster sugar
1 tsp fast-action dried yeast
pinch of salt
1 egg
1 quantity crème pâtissière (see page 19)

For the glaze

30g (1oz) butter
20g (³/₄oz) caster sugar
1 tbsp clear honey
1 tbsp double cream
30g (1oz) slivered almonds
1 tsp lemon juice

METHOD

1 Sift the flour into a bowl. Quickly rub in the butter with your fingertips, then add the sugar, yeast, and salt and mix well. Beat in the egg and add enough water to make a soft dough.

2 Knead the dough on a floured surface for 5–10 minutes, or until smooth, elastic, and shiny. Put in a clean, oiled bowl, cover with cling film, and leave to rise in a warm place for 45–60 minutes, or until doubled in size.

3 Grease the sandwich tin and line with baking parchment. Knock back the dough and roll it out into a circle to fit the tin. Push it into the tin and cover with cling film. Leave to rise for 20 minutes.

4 To make the glaze, melt the butter in a small pan, then add the sugar, honey, and cream. Cook over low heat until the sugar has dissolved, then increase the heat and bring to the boil. Allow to simmer for 3 minutes, then remove the pan from the heat and add the almonds and lemon juice. Allow to cool.

5 Preheat the oven to 190°C (375°F/Gas 5). Carefully spread the glaze over the dough, leave to rise for a further 10 minutes, then bake for 20–25 minutes, ensuring it doesn't get too dark on the top. Allow to cool in the tin for 30 minutes, then carefully transfer to a wire rack.

6 Slice the cake in half. Spread a thick layer of crème pâtissière on the bottom half, then place the almond layer on top. Transfer to a serving plate.

serves 8–10

**prep 30 mins,
plus rising
• cook 20–25
mins**

**20cm (8in)
round
sandwich tin**

Chocolate cake with chocolate fudge icing

A perennial favourite for birthdays and special treats.

INGREDIENTS

200g (7oz) self-raising flour
25g (scant 1oz) cocoa powder
4 large eggs
225g (8oz) caster sugar
225g (8oz) unsalted butter, at room temperature
1 tsp pure vanilla extract
1 tsp baking powder

For the chocolate fudge icing

45g (1½oz) cocoa powder
150g (5½oz) icing sugar
45g (1½oz) unsalted butter, melted
3 tbsp milk

METHOD

1 Preheat the oven to 180°C (350°F/Gas 4). Grease 2 sandwich tins, then line with baking parchment. Sift the flour and cocoa powder into a large bowl then add all the other cake ingredients. Mix together with a wooden spoon, an electric hand whisk, or mixer for a few minutes until well combined. Mix in 2 tbsp of warm water from the kettle so the mixture is soft enough to drop easily off the spoon or whisk. Divide evenly between the sandwich tins, and smooth the tops.

2 Bake for 35–40 minutes, or until risen and firm to the touch, then leave to cool in the tins for 5 minutes before turning out to cool on wire racks.

3 Meanwhile, make the icing. Sift the cocoa powder and icing sugar into a bowl, add the butter and milk, and mix until smooth and well combined. Add a little extra milk if the mixture is too thick – you need to be able to spread it easily. Spread over the tops of the two cooled cakes, then sandwich them together.

serves 8–12

prep 20 mins
• cook 35–40 mins

two x 20cm
(8in) round
sandwich tins

freeze, before
icing, for up to
3 months

Chocolate log

A roulade with the classic pairing of dark chocolate and raspberry.

INGREDIENTS

3 eggs
85g (3oz) caster sugar
85g (3oz) plain flour
3 tbsp cocoa powder
$^1/_2$ tsp baking powder
icing sugar, for dusting

For the filling and icing

200ml (7fl oz) double cream
140g (5oz) dark chocolate, chopped
3 tbsp raspberry jam

METHOD

1 Preheat the oven to 180°C (350°F/Gas 4). Grease and line the Swiss roll tin with a piece of baking parchment.

2 In a large bowl, whisk the eggs with the sugar and 1 tbsp of water for 5 minutes, or until pale and light; the mixture should hold a trail. Sift the flour, cocoa powder, and baking powder on to the beaten eggs, then carefully and quickly fold in with a metal spoon.

3 Pour the cake mixture into the lined tin, level the top, and bake for 12 minutes. It is ready when the top is springy to the touch.

4 Meanwhile, to make the icing, pour the cream into a small saucepan, bring to the boil, then remove from the heat. Add the chopped chocolate, and leave it to melt, stirring occasionally. Allow the mixture to cool and thicken.

5 When the cake is ready, turn it out on to a new piece of baking parchment. Peel off the parchment the cake was cooked on from the base of the cake and discard. Roll the cake up, while still hot, keeping the parchment inside. Leave to cool.

6 To assemble the log, carefully unroll the cake, and spread the raspberry jam over the surface. Spread a third of the icing over the raspberry jam, and roll it up again. Place the roll on a board, seam-side down. Spread the rest of the icing all over the top, sides, and ends of the cake. Use a fork to create ridges down the length and ends of the cake. Transfer to a serving plate. Just before serving, dust with icing sugar.

serves 10

**prep 30 mins
• cook 15 mins**

**20 × 28cm
(8 × 11in)
Swiss roll tin**

**freeze for
up to 6 months**

Chocolate Amaretti roulade

Crushed Amaretti biscuits add crunch to this indulgent roulade.

INGREDIENTS

6 large eggs, separated
150g (5½oz) caster sugar
50g (1¾oz) cocoa powder
icing sugar, to dust
300ml (10fl oz) double cream or whipping cream
2–3 tbsp Amaretto or brandy
20 Amaretti biscuits, crushed, plus 2 extra
50g (1¾oz) dark chocolate

METHOD

1 Preheat the oven to 180°C (350°F/Gas 4). Line the Swiss roll tin with baking parchment. Put the egg yolks and sugar in a large heatproof bowl set over a pan of simmering water and whisk vigorously with a balloon whisk or with an electric hand whisk until very pale, thick, and creamy. This will take about 10 minutes. Remove from the heat. Put the egg whites in a large clean, dry glass or metal mixing bowl and whisk with a clean whisk until soft peaks form.

2 Sift the cocoa powder into the egg yolk mixture and very gently fold in along with the egg whites. Pour into the tin and smooth into the corners. Bake for 20 minutes, or until just firm to the touch. Allow the tin to cool slightly before carefully turning the sponge out face down on to a sheet of baking parchment well dusted with icing sugar. Remove the tin from the sponge, but leave the parchment, and allow to cool for 30 minutes.

3 Put the cream in a mixing bowl and whisk with an electric hand whisk until soft peaks form. Peel the parchment the cake was cooked on off the sponge, trim the sides to neaten them, then drizzle over the Amaretto or brandy. Spread with the cream, scatter with the crushed Amaretti biscuits, then grate over most of the chocolate.

4 Starting from one of the short sides, roll the roulade up, using the parchment to help keep it tightly together. Place on a serving plate with the join underneath. Crumble over the extra biscuits, grate over the remaining chocolate, and dust with a little icing sugar.

serves 8

prep 30 mins
• cook 20 mins

23 x 33cm
(9 x 13in)
Swiss roll tin

Sachertorte

This sumptuous cake was invented in 1832 by Franz Sacher, in Vienna.

INGREDIENTS

250g (9oz) unsalted butter,
    at room temperature
250g (9oz) caster sugar
250g (9oz) dark chocolate, melted
½ tsp pure vanilla extract
5 eggs, separated
250g (9oz) plain flour
6–8 tbsp apricot glaze, or sieved apricot jam

For the chocolate glaze

300ml (10fl oz) whipping cream
200g (7oz) dark chocolate, chopped
few drops of pure vanilla extract

METHOD

1 Preheat the oven to 180°C (350°F/Gas 4). Line the cake tin with baking parchment.

2 To make the cake, beat together the butter and the sugar until the mixture is light and fluffy, then beat in the chocolate and vanilla extract. Beat in the egg yolks, one at a time, then fold in the plain flour with a metal spoon.

3 In a separate, large clean, dry glass or metal bowl, whisk the egg whites until stiff. Spoon a little of the egg whites into the chocolate mixture, and mix in to lighten it slightly, then carefully fold in the remaining egg whites. Pour the mixture into the lined cake tin and level the surface.

4 Bake the cake in the centre of the oven for 45–60 minutes, or until it feels just firm to the touch in the centre and a skewer inserted into it comes out clean. Remove from the oven, and place the tin on a wire rack. Leave the cake to cool in the tin.

5 To make the chocolate glaze, pour the cream into a small saucepan, and bring it to the boil. Place the chopped chocolate in a bowl, then pour in the cream, and stir until the chocolate melts. Add a few drops of vanilla extract. Leave the chocolate mixture to cool slightly, until it reaches a coating consistency, stirring occasionally. If the glaze cools too much and becomes too thick, it can be gently re-warmed.

6 Heat the apricot glaze in a small saucepan until runny. Slice the cake in half horizontally, and spread half with a thin layer of the apricot glaze, then sandwich the 2 halves together again. Spread the remaining glaze over the top and sides of the cake.

7 Place the cake on a wire rack over a plate or tray. Reserve 3 tbsp of the glaze. Pour the rest of the glaze over the cake, using a palette knife to spread it evenly over the sides. Any glaze that runs off on to the plate or tray may be re-used. Leave the cake in a cool place until the glaze has set.

8 Beat the reserved glaze briefly, re-warming it slightly if it is very thick, then use it to fill a piping bag fitted with a plain nozzle. Pipe the word "Sacher" across the top of the cake.

serves 8–12

prep 40 mins
• cook 45–60
mins

23cm (9in)
round cake tin
• piping bag

freeze,
undecorated,
for up to
3 months

Marble cake

The marbled effect is a clever swirl of plain and chocolate batters.

INGREDIENTS

300g (10oz) unsalted butter,
  at room temperature
300g (10oz) caster sugar
few drops of pure vanilla extract
pinch of salt
5 eggs
375g (13oz) plain flour
4 tsp baking powder
4 tbsp milk
20g ($^3/_4$oz) cocoa powder
icing sugar, for dusting

METHOD

1 Preheat the oven to 180°C (350°F/Gas 4). Grease the kugelhopf mould or rectangular tin.

2 Place the butter in a bowl and beat until smooth using a wooden spoon or an electric hand whisk. Gradually stir in the sugar, vanilla extract, and salt until thickened and smooth. Add the eggs, one at a time, whisking vigorously each time.

3 Sift and fold in the flour and baking powder into the butter and egg mixture in 2 stages, adding 2 tbsp of the milk in between.

4 Spoon $^2/_3$ of the mixture into the prepared tin. Sift the cocoa powder into the rest of the mixture with the remaining milk and fold in until mixed. Spoon the cocoa batter on top of the plain, and swirl to create a marbled pattern. Bake for 1 hour, or until risen and golden brown.

5 Leave to cool in the tin for 10 minutes, then transfer to a wire rack. Dust with icing sugar.

serves 12

prep 30 mins
• cook 1 hr

23cm (9in)
kugelhopf
mould or
35 × 11cm
(14 × 4½in)
rectangular tin

Pecan, coffee, and maple cake

This rich, sweet cake is perfect with coffee.

INGREDIENTS

225g (8oz) self-raising flour
175g (6oz) caster sugar
175g (6oz) unsalted butter, at room temperature
3 large eggs
2 tbsp espresso, or strong coffee
75g (2$\frac{1}{2}$oz) pecans, chopped

For the icing

50g (1$\frac{3}{4}$oz) unsalted butter
1 tbsp maple syrup
200g (7oz) icing sugar
2 tbsp espresso, or strong coffee made with water
20 pecan halves or 50g (1$\frac{3}{4}$oz) chopped pecans, to decorate

METHOD

1 Preheat the oven to 180°C (350°F/Gas 4). Lightly grease the 2 sandwich tins and line the bases with baking parchment. Sift the flour into a large bowl. Add the sugar, butter, eggs, and coffee, and mix until well combined. The mixture should drop easily off the spoon or whisk when it is gently tapped on the edge of the bowl. Add a little extra coffee if it seems too thick. Stir in the pecans, divide the mixture between the tins, and level the tops.

2 Bake for 35–40 minutes, or until risen, firm to the touch, and slightly shrunken from the sides of the tins. Leave to cool for 5 minutes in the tins, then transfer to a wire rack to cool completely.

3 Meanwhile, make the icing. Melt the butter and maple syrup together in a small pan. Sift the icing sugar into a bowl, add the butter and syrup mixture along with the coffee and mix until thick, smooth, and a creamy coffee colour. Spread over the tops of the two cooled cakes, then sandwich together. Decorate around the edge of the top with pecans.

serves 8

**prep 15 mins
• cook 35–40 mins**

**two 18cm
(7in) round
sandwich tins**

**freeze, before
icing, for up to
2 months**

Honey cake

The unusual pairing of prunes and sweetened sour cream makes this a novel – and delicious-looking – variation on a Russian honey cake.

INGREDIENTS

100g (3^1/$_2$oz) unsalted butter
75ml (2^1/$_2$fl oz) clear honey
2 large eggs
350g (12oz) plain flour
^{1}/$_2$ tsp baking powder

1 Earl Grey teabag
500g (1lb 2oz) prunes, pitted
200g (7oz) golden caster sugar
300ml (10fl oz) sour cream

METHOD

1 Place the butter and honey in a bowl and cream together thoroughly. Beat in the eggs, then fold in the flour and baking powder with a metal spoon. Mix together to form a dough. Wrap the dough in cling film and refrigerate for 2 hours.

2 Remove the dough from the refrigerator and leave to come to room temperature – about 30 minutes.

3 Make the tea by pouring 100ml (3^1/$_2$fl oz) boiling water over the teabag in a jug. Leave for 3 minutes, then strain the tea into a small saucepan. Add the prunes and half the sugar. Bring to the boil, then remove from the heat and leave to cool.

4 Preheat the oven to 180°C (350°F/Gas 4). Line a large baking tray with baking parchment. Divide the dough into 6 equal balls, then roll out each ball on a lightly floured surface to a thickness of about 3mm (^{1}/$_8$in) – like a thick pancake. Cut them into large circles, using a 14cm (5^1/$_2$in) diameter bowl or plate to cut around.

5 Place 2 rounds on the prepared baking tray and bake for 5–10 minutes, or until golden. Remove from the oven and transfer to a wire rack to cool. When the baking tray is cool, repeat with the remaining rounds.

6 Stir the sour cream in a bowl with the remaining half of the sugar until the mixture is smooth. Place the rounds separately on a plate or clean work surface and spread each generously with the sweetened sour cream.

7 Assemble the cake on a serving plate. Start with a cream-topped round, spoon a layer of prunes and tea syrup over it, and top with another cream-topped round. Repeat until all the cream-topped rounds have been used. Finish with a generous drizzle of tea syrup and prunes on the top. Carefully cover and leave to sit for 2 hours before serving.

PREPARE AHEAD The cake can be stored for up to 2 days in the refrigerator.

serves 6

prep 20 mins, plus chilling and assembling • cook 30 mins

allow 2 hrs for chilling, and 2 hrs for sitting

large baking tray • 14cm (5½in) diameter bowl or plate

freeze the uncooked dough for up to 3 months

Chocolate almond cake

A dense, moist cake with a rich ganache topping.

INGREDIENTS

plain flour, to dust
115g (4oz) dark chocolate, broken into pieces
115g (4oz) unsalted butter, at room temperature
140g (5oz) caster sugar
3 eggs, separated
60g (2oz) ground almonds
30g (1oz) white breadcrumbs
$1/2$ tsp baking powder
1 tsp almond extract
1 tbsp brandy or rum (optional)

For the ganache

115g (4oz) plain chocolate
60g (2oz) unsalted butter

METHOD

1 Preheat the oven to 180°C (350°F/Gas 4). Grease the tin and line the bottom of the tin with baking parchment, then dust with plain flour.

2 Place the chocolate pieces in a heatproof bowl over a saucepan of simmering water, and melt the chocolate, stirring occasionally. Don't let the bowl touch the water. Set aside.

3 Beat the butter and sugar together until pale and creamy. Add the egg yolks one at a time, beating well after each addition. Beat in the chocolate. Add the almonds, breadcrumbs, baking powder, almond extract, and brandy, if using, and fold in gently.

4 Whisk the egg whites in a large clean, dry glass or metal bowl until soft peaks form. Fold into the cake mixture, then spoon into the tin.

5 Bake for 25 minutes, or until a skewer inserted into the centre comes out clean. Remove from the oven and cool on a wire rack.

6 To make the ganache, melt the chocolate and butter together in a bowl over a saucepan of simmering water, stirring to combine. Remove from the heat and cool slightly. Using a palette knife, spread the ganache over the top of the cake. Allow to set.

serves 6–8

prep 30 mins
• cook 25 mins

18cm (7in)
round
loose-
bottomed
cake tin

freeze for
up to 1 month

FRUITY CAKES

Light fruitcake

In contrast to traditional heavy fruitcakes, this recipe is a good everyday bake.

INGREDIENTS

175g (6oz) unsalted butter, at room temperature
175g (6oz) light soft brown sugar
3 large eggs
250g (9oz) self-raising flour, sifted
2–3 tbsp milk
300g (10oz) mixed dried fruit (use a luxury mix if possible)

METHOD

1 Preheat the oven to 180°C (350°F/Gas 4). Line the base and sides of the tin with baking parchment. In a bowl, beat the butter and sugar together with an electric hand whisk or a wooden spoon until pale and creamy, then beat in the eggs, one at a time, adding a little of the flour after each one. Stir in the rest of the flour and the milk – the mixture should drop easily off the beaters or spoon. Add the dried fruit and mix until well combined.

2 Spoon the mixture into the tin, level the top, and bake for 1¹/₂–1³/₄ hours, or until firm to the touch and a skewer inserted into the middle of the cake comes out clean. Leave in the tin to cool completely.

serves 8–12

prep 25 mins
• cook 1 hr
30–45 mins

20cm (8in)
deep round
cake tin

freeze for
up to 3 months

Apricot cake

This light-as-a-feather cake has a winning combination of apricot and cinnamon flavours and a crunchy sugary topping.

INGREDIENTS

75g (2^1/$_2$oz) ready-to-eat dried apricots,
  chopped into 1cm (^{1}/$_2$in) pieces
6 large eggs, separated
115g (4oz) caster sugar, plus 1 tbsp,
  to sprinkle
juice of 1 lemon
140g (5oz) plain flour, sifted
30g (1oz) unsalted butter
^{1}/$_2$ tsp ground cinnamon

METHOD

1 Preheat the oven to 180°C (350°F/Gas 4). Grease the springform cake tin and line with baking parchment. Place the chopped apricots in a bowl with enough cold water to cover, and leave to soak for 20 minutes. Drain and set aside.

2 Place the egg yolks and sugar in a large bowl, and beat with an electric hand whisk for about 5 minutes until thick, creamy, and pale, and tripled in volume. Add the lemon juice and beat to combine. Fold in the flour thoroughly with a metal spoon, then set aside.

3 Place the egg whites in a large clean, dry glass or metal bowl and beat, using an electric whisk with clean beaters, until the whites form soft peaks. Fold half the beaten egg white into the cake mixture, then fold in the remaining half.

4 Transfer ^{1}/$_3$ of the mixture to the prepared tin, level it, then layer with ^{1}/$_3$ of the apricots. Add another ^{1}/$_3$ of the cake mixture, and top with another ^{1}/$_3$ of the apricots. Spread the final ^{1}/$_3$ of the cake mixture on top, followed by the remaining apricots.

5 Melt the butter in a small saucepan over a gentle heat, then drizzle over the top of the cake mixture. Mix the cinnamon with the remaining 1 tbsp of sugar in a small bowl, and sprinkle evenly over the top of the cake mixture.

6 Bake in the middle of the oven for 40–45 minutes, or until the top is golden and springy, and a skewer inserted into the centre of the cake comes out clean. Remove from the oven and leave to cool completely in the tin – the cake will shrink from the sides of the tin – then release from the springform tin.

GOOD WITH Berries and cream as a dessert.

serves 6

prep 15 mins,
plus soaking
• cook 45 mins

eat on the day
of making

23cm (9in)
round
springform
cake tin
• electric hand
whisk

Sticky lemon cake

Fresh lemon juice and yogurt give this cake a fresh taste and moist texture.

INGREDIENTS
175g (6oz) unsalted butter, at room temperature
250g (9oz) caster sugar
2 lemons
3 eggs
75g (2^1/$_2$oz) plain flour
2 tsp baking powder
150g (5^1/$_2$oz) ground almonds
150g (5^1/$_2$oz) natural yogurt

METHOD
1 Preheat the oven to 170°C (325°F/Gas 3). Grease the cake tin and line the base with baking parchment. Set aside.

2 Cream together the butter and 150g (5^1/$_2$oz) caster sugar in a large bowl. Grate the zest from both lemons, add to the bowl, and mix together. Gradually beat in the eggs, one at a time. If the mixture shows signs of curdling, add 1 tsp of flour.

3 Mix the flour, baking powder, and ground almonds together. Sift into a separate bowl, then fold into the butter and eggs with a metal spoon. Stir in the juice of 1 lemon and the yogurt. Pour the mixture into the tin.

4 Bake for 40 minutes or until the centre of the cake is just firm to the touch. Do not open the oven door for the first 20 minutes.

5 Remove the cake from the oven and leave to cool in the tin. Heat the remaining sugar and the juice from the remaining lemon in a saucepan. Pierce the cake several times with a skewer, then drizzle the syrup over the cake. Leave to cool before removing the cake from the tin.

serves 8

**prep 15 mins
• cook 40 mins**

**20cm (8in)
deep round
cake tin**

FRUITY CAKES

Cherry and almond cake

Fresh, juicy cherries make this sponge a delicious contrast to dried-fruit cakes.

INGREDIENTS

150g (5¹/₂oz) unsalted butter, at room temperature
150g (5¹/₂oz) caster sugar
2 large eggs, lightly beaten
250g (9oz) self-raising flour, sifted
1 tsp baking powder
150g (5¹/₂oz) ground almonds
1 tsp pure vanilla extract
75ml (2¹/₂fl oz) whole milk
400g (14oz) pitted cherries
25g (scant 1oz) whole blanched almonds, chopped (lengthways looks attractive)

METHOD

1 Preheat the oven to 180°C (350°F/Gas 4). Lightly grease the cake tin and line the base with baking parchment. In a bowl, beat together the butter and sugar with an electric hand whisk or wooden spoon until pale and creamy. Beat in the eggs one at a time, adding 1 tbsp of the flour before adding the second egg.

2 Mix in the remaining flour, baking powder, ground almonds, and vanilla extract. Stir in the milk – the mixture should drop easily off the beaters of the whisk. Mix in half the cherries, then spoon the mixture into the tin and smooth the top. Scatter the remaining cherries over the top, followed by the chopped almonds.

3 Bake for 1¹/₂–1³/₄ hours, or until golden and firm to the touch. The exact cooking time will depend on how juicy the cherries are. To test, insert a skewer into the cake – if there is uncooked mixture on it, put the cake back into the oven for another 5 minutes and test again. If the surface of the cake starts to brown too much before it is fully cooked, cover with foil. When cooked, leave to cool in the tin for 5 minutes, then transfer to a wire rack to cool completely before serving.

serves 8–10

prep 20 mins • cook 1 hr 30–45 mins

20cm (8in) deep round loose-bottomed or springform cake tin

70

Tropical fruit and ginger cake

This delicious sticky cake offers a new twist on traditional gingerbread-type cakes

INGREDIENTS

100g (3½oz) golden syrup
100g (3½oz) black treacle
50g (1¾oz) dried mango, thinly sliced
50g (1¾oz) dried pineapple, thinly sliced
50g (1¾oz) pitted dates, roughly chopped
125g (4½oz) unsalted butter, at
   room temperature
125g (4½oz) golden caster sugar
2 large eggs, beaten

275g (9½oz) plain flour
1½ tsp bicarbonate of soda
1 tsp salt
1 tsp ground cinnamon
1 tsp ground ginger

For the syrup

grated zest and juice of 1 lemon
50g (1¾oz) golden caster sugar

METHOD

1 Place the syrup, treacle, and 225ml (7½fl oz) water in a large saucepan and bring to the boil. Add the mango, pineapple, and dates, and simmer gently for 5 minutes. Pour the fruit mixture on to a tray or shallow plate, and leave to cool at room temperature for about 15 minutes.

2 Preheat the oven to 180°C (350°F/Gas 4). Grease the springform cake tin and line with baking parchment.

3 Place the butter and sugar in a large bowl and cream with an electric whisk or wooden spoon until light and fluffy. Beat in the eggs gradually. Sift over the flour, bicarbonate of soda, salt, cinnamon, and ginger, then add the cooled fruit mixture. Fold in gently with a metal spoon.

4 Transfer the mixture to the prepared cake tin and bake in the centre of the oven for 50 minutes, or until the cake feels firm in the centre or a skewer inserted into the centre comes out clean. Remove from the oven and leave in the tin while you make the syrup.

5 To make the syrup, place the lemon zest and juice, 60ml (2fl oz) water, and the sugar in a small saucepan. Heat gently to melt the sugar, then boil for 3–4 minutes to reduce to a slightly sticky syrup.

6 Prick the top of the cake all over with a skewer, then pour the hot syrup over the surface, letting it soak into the holes. Leave to cool completely in the tin before turning out.

PREPARE AHEAD The cake can be stored for up to 5 days in an airtight tin.

serves 8

prep 20 mins
• cook 1 hr

23cm (9in)
deep round
springform
cake tin

freeze for
up to 3 months

Orange and pistachio cake

Yogurt gives this zesty, nutty cake a dense, moist texture.

INGREDIENTS

175g (6oz) unsalted butter, at room temperature
175g (6oz) caster sugar
2 eggs
175g (6oz) self-raising flour
175g (6oz) Greek yogurt
75g (2$\frac{1}{2}$oz) pistachio nuts, finely chopped
75g (2$\frac{1}{2}$oz) blanched almonds, finely chopped
grated zest and juice of 1 orange
grated zest and juice of 1 lemon
1 tsp baking powder
icing sugar, to dust
mascarpone, to serve

METHOD

1 Preheat the oven to 180°C (350°F/Gas 4). Lightly grease the cake tin and line the base with baking parchment. Put the butter and sugar in a mixing bowl until pale and creamy. Whisking all the time, add the eggs one at a time, along with a little of the flour to stop the mixture curdling.

2 Add the yogurt, pistachio nuts, almonds, orange and lemon zest and juice, and mix well to form a smooth batter. Sift in the remaining flour and the baking powder and carefully fold in. Pour the mixture into the tin.

3 Bake in the oven for 40 minutes, or until a skewer inserted into the centre of the cake comes out clean. Remove from the oven and leave to cool in the tin for 10 minutes, then release from the tin and leave to cool completely. Sift a little icing sugar over the top of the cake, then slice and serve with spoonfuls of mascarpone.

serves 6

prep 15 mins
• cook 40 mins

20cm (8in)
round
springform
cake tin

freeze for
up to 3 months

Carrot cake

Always popular, this cake has a hint of spice.

INGREDIENTS
75g (2$^{1}/_{2}$oz) wholemeal self-raising flour
1 tsp ground allspice
$^{1}/_{2}$ tsp baking powder
$^{1}/_{2}$ tsp ground ginger
2 carrots, peeled and coarsely grated
75g (2$^{1}/_{2}$oz) light soft brown sugar
50g (1$^{3}/_{4}$oz) sultanas
2 eggs, beaten
3 tbsp fresh orange juice
75g (2$^{1}/_{2}$oz) unsalted butter, at room temperature
150g (5$^{1}/_{2}$oz) cream cheese
1 tbsp icing sugar
lemon zest, to garnish

METHOD
1 Preheat the oven to 190°C (375°F/Gas 5). Grease the cake tin and line the base with baking parchment. Sift the flour, allspice, baking powder, and ginger into a large bowl, tipping in any bran left in the sieve. Add the carrots, sugar, and sultanas, then stir to mix.

2 Add the eggs, 1 tbsp of the orange juice, and the butter. Stir together until well blended.

3 Stand the prepared tin on a baking tray, pour in the cake mixture, and level the surface using a palette knife. Bake for 20 minutes, or until a skewer inserted into the centre comes out clean. Let stand in the tin for 10 minutes, to cool.

4 Run the palette knife around the sides, invert on to a wire rack, peel off the paper, and leave to cool. Split the cake horizontally for layers.

5 Beat the cream cheese with the remaining orange juice and sweeten to taste with the icing sugar. Spread the icing in the centre and over the top of the cake, and decorate with strips of lemon zest.

serves 8

**prep 15 mins
• cook 20 mins**

**20cm (8in)
round cake tin**

FRUITY CAKES

Almond and orange cake

This cake does not need flour or butter, so is great for restricted diets.

INGREDIENTS
200g (7oz) carrots, peeled
4 large eggs, separated
few drops of pure vanilla extract
grated zest and juice of 1 orange
150g (5^1/$_2$oz) caster sugar
1 tbsp orange juice, or orange- or almond-flavoured liqueur
150g (5^1/$_2$oz) ground almonds
raspberries, to garnish
icing sugar, for dusting

METHOD
1 Preheat the oven to 160°C (325°F/Gas 3). Line the cake tin with baking parchment. Cook the carrots in a little water until tender, then drain, cool slightly, and use a food processor or blender to blend to a purée with the orange juice.

2 Whisk the egg yolks in a large bowl with the vanilla and grated orange zest. Gradually add the sugar, whisking until it becomes thick and pale. Fold in the carrot purée and ground almonds.

3 In a clean, dry glass or metal bowl, whisk the egg whites until stiff, then fold them into the yolk mixture. Pour into the prepared cake tin and bake for 1 hour, or until a skewer inserted into the centre comes out clean.

4 Cool in the tin for 10 minutes, then transfer the cake to a wire rack and leave to cool completely. Pile on the raspberries and sift icing sugar over the top to serve.

GOOD WITH Fresh fruit, such as raspberries, blackberries, blueberries, or redcurrants, and a spoonful of Greek yogurt or whipped cream.

serves 8

prep 10 mins
• cook 1 hr

20cm (8in)
deep round
cake tin
• food
processor
or blender

Coconut and lime cake

Layers of tangy lime and coconut sponge and cream cheese icing make this cake an attractive centrepiece that your guests will love.

INGREDIENTS
225g (8oz) self-raising flour
225g (8oz) caster sugar
225g (8oz) unsalted butter, at room temperature
4 large eggs, lightly beaten
50g (1³/₄oz) desiccated coconut
grated zest of 1 lime
2 tbsp lime juice

For the icing
100g (3¹/₂oz) icing sugar
grated zest of 1 lime
2 tbsp lime juice
300g (10oz) cream cheese, at room temperature
15g (¹/₂oz) toasted desiccated coconut, to decorate

METHOD

1 Preheat the oven to 180°C (350°F/Gas 4). Lightly grease the tin and line the base with baking parchment. Sift the flour into a large bowl, add the caster sugar, butter, and eggs and mix until well combined. Mix in the coconut, lime zest, and lime juice. Spoon the batter into the tin and level the top. Bake for 1–1¹/₄ hours, or until risen and firm to the touch. Leave to cool for 5 minutes in the tin, then cool completely on a wire rack. Carefully divide the cake into three equal layers using a serrated knife.

2 To make the icing, sift the icing sugar into a bowl, add the lime zest, lime juice, and cream cheese, and whisk until the mixture starts to thicken. Taste to make sure it is sweet enough. Add more icing sugar if it isn't. Spread over the three layers of the cake, then sandwich them together. Scatter the toasted coconut over the top to decorate.

serves 8

prep 20 mins
• cook
1–1¹/₄ hrs

18cm (7in)
deep round
cake tin

freeze, before
icing, for up to
3 months

Apple streusel cake

German in origin, streusel is a sweet, sometimes spiced, crumb mixture.

INGREDIENTS

125g (4¹/₂oz) plain flour
125g (4¹/₂oz) unsalted butter, at room temperature
125g (4¹/₂oz) caster sugar
1 tsp ground cinnamon
2 large eggs, lightly beaten
¹/₂ tsp vanilla extract
1 Bramley apple, peeled, cored, and cut into chunks
50g (1³/₄oz) sultanas

For the streusel topping

75g (2¹/₂oz) butter, cubed
100g (3¹/₂oz) plain flour
25g (scant 1oz) ground almonds
50g (1³/₄oz) caster sugar or light soft brown sugar
1 tsp ground cinnamon

METHOD

1 Preheat the oven to 180°C (350°F/Gas 4). Lightly grease and line the cake tin with baking parchment. Sift the flour into a bowl, add the butter, sugar, cinnamon, eggs, and vanilla extract, and mix until pale, creamy, and well combined. Spoon the mixture into the tin and level the top. Scatter with the apple and sultanas.

2 In another bowl, rub the cubed butter for the topping into the flour with your fingertips until the mixture resembles breadcrumbs. Stir in the ground almonds, sugar, and cinnamon. Scatter the mixture over the fruit in the tin and level the top, pressing down slightly. Bake for 1¹/₄ hours, or until a skewer inserted into the cake comes out clean with no trace of uncooked cake mixture (it will probably be a bit damp from the fruit, though). Leave to cool in the tin for 20 minutes and serve warm, or leave to cool completely.

GOOD WITH Custard, ice cream, or cream.

serves 8

prep 20 mins
• cook 1 hr
15 mins

20cm (8in)
round
loose-
bottomed or
springform
cake tin

Tropical angel cake

Exotic fruits are a perfect partner to this coconut-flavoured angel cake.

INGREDIENTS

4 large egg whites
$^1/_2$ tsp cream of tartar
150g (5$^1/_2$oz) caster sugar
50g (1$^3/_4$oz) plain flour
10g ($^1/_4$oz) cornflour
25g (scant 1oz) desiccated coconut

For the topping

200g (7oz) Greek yogurt
200g (7oz) mixed peeled and chopped tropical fruit,
  such as pineapple and mango
seeds and pulp from 2 passion fruits
lime zest, to decorate

METHOD

1 Preheat the oven to 190°C (375°F/Gas 5). Put the egg whites, cream of tartar, and 1 tbsp cold water in a large clean, dry glass or metal mixing bowl and whisk with a balloon whisk, or an electric whisk or mixer, until the mixture forms stiff peaks. Whisk in the sugar, 1 tbsp at a time, until the mixture is stiff and shiny.

2 Sift in the flour and cornflour and gently fold in with the coconut until well combined. Carefully spoon into the tin and smooth the top, pressing down gently so there are no air spaces left. Bake for 15 minutes, then reduce the oven temperature to 180°C (350°F/Gas 4), and bake for a further 15 minutes, until the mixture is firm to the touch and golden brown.

3 Place the tin upside-down on a wire rack and leave until completely cold, then carefully ease the cake out of the tin with a round-bladed knife or small metal spatula, and place on a serving plate.

4 To make the topping, beat the yogurt lightly so it is smooth and creamy, then spoon into the centre of the cake. Top with the fruit, then drizzle over the passion fruit seeds. Finish by scattering over the lime zest.

serves 6–8

prep 15 mins
• cook 30 mins

1.2 x 1.5-litre
(2 x 2¾-pints)
savarin
ring mould

Celebration cake

This moist, rich fruit cake is ideal for Christmas, weddings, and christenings.

INGREDIENTS

200g (7oz) sultanas
400g (14oz) raisins
350g (12oz) prunes, chopped
350g (12oz) glacé cherries
2 small dessert apples, peeled,
    cored, and finely chopped
600ml (1 pint) cider
4 tsp mixed spice
200g (7oz) unsalted butter, at
    room temperature

175g (6oz) dark brown sugar
3 eggs, beaten
150g (5$^{1}/_{2}$oz) ground almonds
300g (10oz) plain flour
2 tsp baking powder
400g ready-made marzipan icing
3 large egg whites, plus 1 extra for the berries
500g (1lb 2oz) icing sugar
mixed fresh berries, to decorate
caster sugar, for frosting

METHOD

1 Place the sultanas, raisins, prunes, glacé cherries, chopped apple, cider, and spice in a saucepan, bring slowly to simmering point over a medium-low heat, cover, and simmer for 20 minutes, or until most of the liquid has been absorbed.

2 Remove from the heat, and leave to rest overnight at room temperature.

3 Preheat the oven to 160°C (325°F/Gas 3). Double-line the cake tin with baking parchment. In a large bowl, cream the butter and sugar together until pale and fluffy, then add the eggs, a little at a time.

4 Fold in the fruit and ground almonds, then sift the flour and baking powder, and fold into the mixture.

5 Spoon the mixture into the prepared tin, cover with foil, and bake for 2$^{1}/_{2}$ hours, or until a skewer inserted into the centre of the cake comes out clean. Leave to cool.

6 Cover with the marzipan icing. Place the egg whites in a clean, dry glass or metal bowl and stir in the icing sugar. Whisk for 10 minutes until stiff, then spread on top of the marzipan. To decorate, make frosted berries by dipping fresh berries in beaten egg white, then in caster sugar, and leaving to dry.

serves 16

prep 25 mins,
plus soaking
• cook 2 hrs
30 mins

complete steps
1 and 2 a day
ahead to allow
to soak
overnight

20–25cm
(8–10in)
deep square
cake tin

Pear and chocolate cake

This rich, luscious cake is a good choice when you want to impress.

INGREDIENTS

125g (4^1/$_2$oz) unsalted butter, at
    room temperature, plus extra for greasing
175g (6oz) golden caster sugar
4 large eggs, lightly beaten
250g (9oz) self-raising wholemeal flour, sifted
50g (1^3/$_4$oz) cocoa powder
50g (1^3/$_4$oz) dark chocolate, chopped
2 pears, peeled, cored, and chopped
150ml (5fl oz) milk
icing sugar, to dust

METHOD

1 Preheat the oven to 180°C (350°F/Gas 4). Line the base of the springform cake tin with baking parchment, and grease the sides with butter.

2 Cream the butter with the sugar until pale and creamy. Beat the eggs in gradually, adding a little of the flour each time. Fold in the cocoa powder, chopped chocolate, and pears. Add the milk to the mixture, and combine.

3 Pour the batter into the prepared cake tin, place it in the oven, and bake for about 30 minutes, or until firm and springy to the touch. Allow to cool in the tin for 5 minutes, then remove the tin, and transfer the cake to a wire rack to cool completely. Dust with icing sugar before serving.

serves 6–8

prep 30 mins
• cook 30 mins

18cm (7in)
round
springform
cake tin

Toffee-topped banana cake

This big cake is ideal for large family gatherings or other occasions where you need to feed a crowd.

INGREDIENTS
175g (6oz) unsalted butter, at room temperature
175g (6oz) light soft brown sugar
4 eggs, beaten
125g (4^1/$_2$oz) Brazil nuts, chopped
3 large bananas, peeled and mashed
^{1}/$_4$ tsp mixed spice
350g (12oz) self-raising flour
1 tsp baking powder
300ml (10fl oz) plain Greek-style yogurt
    mixed with 1 tbsp clear honey

For the topping
75g (2^1/$_2$oz) unsalted butter
175g (6oz) light soft brown sugar
2 tbsp double cream
75g (2^1/$_2$oz) Brazil nuts, chopped

METHOD
1 Preheat the oven to 180°C (350°F/Gas 4). Grease the cake tin and line with baking parchment.

2 Place the butter and sugar in a large bowl and cream together with a wooden spoon or an electric hand whisk until light and fluffy. Beat in the eggs, a little at a time. Stir in the Brazil nuts, bananas, and spice. Sift the flour and baking powder over the mixture, add the yogurt and honey mixture, and fold in gently with a metal spoon.

3 Transfer to the prepared cake tin, making sure the mixture is evenly distributed, especially into the corners of the tin. Bake for about 1 hour 20 minutes, or until a skewer inserted into the centre of the cake comes out clean. Preheat the grill.

4 For the topping, place the butter, sugar, and cream in a saucepan. Bring to simmering point, stirring well. Remove from the heat and stir in the Brazil nuts.

5 Spread the mixture evenly over the cake, then place the cake under the preheated grill for 1–2 minutes, or until the toffee mixture starts to bubble. Leave to cool completely in the tin before turning releasing the springform.

PREPARE AHEAD The cake can be stored in an airtight container for up to 2 days.

serves 12

prep 15 mins
• cook 1 hr
25 mins

20cm (8in)
deep round
springform tin

Black Forest gâteau

The stunning Black Forest region of Germany is home to this indulgent cake.

INGREDIENTS

6 eggs
175g (6oz) golden caster sugar
125g (4½oz) plain flour
50g (1¾oz) cocoa powder
1 tsp pure vanilla extract

85g (3oz) unsalted butter, melted
600ml (1 pint) double cream
2 x 425g can pitted black cherries
4 tbsp Kirsch
150g (5½oz) dark chocolate, grated

METHOD

1 Preheat the oven to 180°C (350°F/Gas 4). Lightly grease and line the bottom of the tin with baking parchment. Put the eggs and sugar into a large heatproof bowl, and place over a saucepan filled with simmering water. Don't let the bowl touch the water. Whisk until the mixture is pale and thick, and will hold a trail. Remove from the heat and whisk for another 5 minutes, or until cooled slightly.

2 Sift the flour and cocoa together, and fold into the egg mixture using a large metal spoon or a spatula. Fold in the vanilla extract and butter. Transfer to the prepared tin, and level the surface. Bake in the oven for 40 minutes, or until risen and just shrinking away a little from the sides. Turn it out on to a wire rack, discard the lining paper, and cover with a clean cloth. Allow the cake to cool completely.

3 Carefully cut the cake into three layers. Drain 1 can of cherries, placing 6 tbsp of the juice into a bowl with the Kirsch. Roughly chop the drained cherries. Drizzle a third of the Kirsch and cherry syrup over each layer of sponge.

4 Whip the cream until it just holds its shape. Place 1 layer of the cake on to a serving plate. Spread a thin layer of cream over the top of the sponge, and scatter with half the chopped cherries. Repeat with layers, and top with the final layer of sponge. Using a palette knife, spread a thin layer of cream around the edges of the cake to cover, and spoon the remaining cream into a piping bag fitted with a star-shaped nozzle.

5 Using a spoon or a palette knife, press the grated chocolate on to the side of the cake. Pipe swirls of cream around the top edge of the cake. Drain the second tin of cherries, and use them to fill the centre of the cake. Scatter any remaining chocolate over the piped cream.

PREPARE AHEAD The cake can be made up to 3 days in advance. Store in the refrigerator until ready to serve.

serves 8

prep 55 mins • cook 40 mins

23cm (9in) round springform cake tin • piping bag

freeze for up to 1 month

LOAF CAKES

Banana bread

A moist cake that keeps well.

INGREDIENTS

250g (9oz) self-raising flour
$\frac{1}{2}$ tsp baking powder
85g (3oz) unsalted butter, plus extra for greasing
150g ($5\frac{1}{2}$oz) light muscovado sugar
3 ripe bananas
100ml ($3\frac{1}{2}$fl oz) plain yogurt
2 eggs
85g (3oz) walnuts, chopped

METHOD

1 Preheat the oven to 180°C (350°F/Gas 4). Grease the loaf tin and line with baking parchment. Sift the flour and baking powder together into a mixing bowl, and rub in the butter with your fingertips until the mixture resembles fine breadcrumbs. Stir in the sugar.

2 Mash the bananas with a fork, then add to the flour with the yogurt, eggs, and walnuts. Beat with a wooden spoon until well combined. Spoon into the loaf tin, level the top, then make a slight dip in the centre.

3 Bake for $1-1\frac{1}{4}$ hours, or until a skewer inserted into the centre comes out clean. Leave to cool in the tin for 5 minutes, then turn out on to a wire rack to cool completely.

PREPARE AHEAD Will keep for at least 1 week in an airtight container.

serves 8–10

prep 15 mins
• cook
$1-1\frac{1}{2}$ hrs

900g (2lb)
loaf tin

Honey loaf

A sweet cake with a delicate taste of honey.

INGREDIENTS

225g (8oz) unsalted butter
115g (4oz) light muscovado sugar
6 tbsp clear honey
4 eggs, lightly beaten
450g (1lb) plain flour
1½ tsp baking powder
1 tsp ground cinnamon

For the icing

115g (4oz) icing sugar
1 tbsp clear honey

METHOD

1 Preheat the oven to 180°C (350°F/Gas 4). Grease and line the bottom of the loaf tin.

2 Beat the butter and sugar with a wooden spoon or electric whisk until they are pale and creamy. Warm the honey in a small pan, then beat into the butter and sugar mixture. Beat in the eggs, a little at a time, beating well after each addition. Add a little flour it the mixture begins to curdle.

3 Sift the flour, baking powder, and cinnamon together, and fold into the cake mixture with a metal spoon. Spoon into the prepared loaf tin and level the top. Bake in the centre of the oven for 50–60 minutes. Check after 40 minutes; if the crust is getting too dark, reduce the heat to 160°C (325°F/Gas 3), and cover the crust with a piece of baking parchment for the remaining time. The cake is cooked when well risen, and if a skewer inserted into the centre comes out clean. Remove from the tin, and place on a wire rack to cool completely.

4 Mix the icing sugar with the honey and 1–2 tbsp of hot water to make a runny glacé icing. Spoon the icing over the top of the cake, allowing it to drizzle down the sides.

serves 10–12

**prep 20 mins
• cook 50–60
mins**

**900g (2lb)
loaf tin**

Lemon, lime, and poppy seed cake

Poppy seeds add a delicate texture to this citrussy loaf cake.

INGREDIENTS

175g (6oz) unsalted butter,
 at room temperature
175g (6oz) caster sugar
3 large eggs, lightly beaten
zest of 1 lemon
zest of 1 lime
1 tbsp lemon juice
175g (6oz) self-raising flour
2 tbsp poppy seeds

For the icing

1 tbsp lemon juice
1 tbsp lime juice
100g (3$^{1}/_{2}$oz) icing sugar

METHOD

1 Preheat the oven to 180°C (350°F/Gas 4). Line the base and sides of the loaf tin with baking parchment. In a large bowl, beat the butter and caster sugar together with a wooden spoon or an electric hand whisk, until light and fluffy. Beat in the eggs a little at a time, then gently fold in the lemon and lime zest, together with the lemon juice. Sift in the flour, then fold in with the poppy seeds.

2 Transfer to the tin and smooth the top. Bake for 1 hour, or until risen, golden, and firm to the touch. Leave to cool in the tin for 5 minutes, then remove and leave to cool completely on a wire rack.

3 Meanwhile, make the icing. Mix the lemon juice with the lime juice in a bowl. Sift in the icing sugar, and combine to make a runny glacé icing. Place a piece of baking parchment under the wire rack to catch the drips, then spoon the icing over the cake, letting it drizzle down the sides. Leave to set before serving.

serves 8–10

**prep 15 mins
• cook 1 hr**

**18 x 9cm
(7 x 3½ in) 2lb
loaf tin**

**freeze, before
icing, for up to
3 months**

Caribbean tea bread

With its flavours of the Caribbean, this is a satisfying cake to serve with an afternoon cup of tea.

INGREDIENTS

2 teabags
125g (4¹/₂oz) mixed dried fruit
50g (1³/₄oz) dried pineapple, cut into small pieces
50g (1³/₄oz) dried mango, cut into small pieces
3 tbsp white rum
100g (3¹/₂oz) dark soft brown sugar
2 large eggs, beaten
100g (3¹/₂oz) unsalted butter, at room temperature
¹/₄ tsp mixed spice
225g (8oz) self-raising flour

METHOD

1 To make the tea, pour 220ml (7¹/₂fl oz) boiling water over the teabags in a jug. Leave to steep for 3 minutes, then remove the teabags, squeeze them out into the jug, and discard.

2 Place the mixed dried fruit, pineapple, and mango in a large bowl, and add the hot tea and rum. Leave to cool to room temperature, then stir and cover with clingfilm. Leave to macerate for at least 8 hours or overnight.

3 The next day, preheat the oven to 160°C (325°F/Gas 3). Lightly grease the loaf tin and line with baking parchment.

4 Add the sugar, eggs, butter, and mixed spice to the fruit, tea, and rum mixture and mix until well combined. Sift the flour over and fold in with a metal spoon. The mixture should have a slightly wet consistency.

5 Transfer the mixture to the prepared tin and bake for 1 hour 15 minutes, or until a skewer inserted into the centre comes out clean. Remove from the oven and leave to cool in the tin for 20 minutes, then transfer to a wire rack to cool completely.

PREPARE AHEAD This will keep for up to 2 days in an airtight container.

serves 6

**prep 20 mins
• cook 1 hr
15 mins**

**macerate for
8 hrs or
overnight**

**450g (1lb)
loaf tin**

**freeze for
up to 3 months**

Banana, cranberry, and walnut loaf

Cranberries and walnuts are a delicious combination in this moist loaf cake.

INGREDIENTS

115g (4oz) unsalted butter, at room temperature
175g (6oz) caster sugar
2 large eggs, beaten
1 tsp milk
300g (10oz) plain flour
$\frac{1}{2}$ tsp salt
1 tsp bicarbonate of soda
1 tsp mixed spice
3 ripe bananas, peeled and mashed
85g (3oz) dried cranberries
60g (2oz) walnuts, roughly chopped

METHOD

1 Preheat the oven to 160°C (325°F/Gas 3). Grease 2 small loaf tins, or 1 large loaf tin and line with baking parchment.

2 Cream the butter and sugar together in a large bowl until pale and creamy. Add the beaten eggs and milk, and mix well.

3 Stir in the flour, salt, bicarbonate of soda, and spice, followed by the bananas, cranberries, and walnuts.

4 Divide the mixture between the two small loaf tins or transfer to the large tin. Bake in the middle of the oven for 45–50 minutes if using the small tins, and for 1–1¼ hours if using the large tin. The cake is cooked when a skewer inserted into the centre comes out clean. Remove from the oven and leave to cool in the tin for 10 minutes, then transfer to a wire rack to cool completely.

PREPARE AHEAD The cake will keep for up to 1 week in an airtight tin.

serves 8–12

prep 20 mins
• cook 50 mins
(small loaves)
or 1 hr 15 mins
(large loaf)

two 450g (1lb)
loaf tins or one
900g (2lb) loaf
tin

freeze for
up to 3 months

Marmalade and ginger loaf

Cinnamon and ginger give this cake a warm, spicy character.

INGREDIENTS

225g (8oz) self-raising flour
175g (6oz) unsalted butter, at room temperature
175g (6oz) caster sugar
3 large eggs, lightly beaten
1 tsp baking powder
1 tsp ground cinnamon
1 tsp ground ginger
150g (5$^{1}/_{2}$oz) thick-cut Seville
  orange marmalade, plus 2 tbsp extra to brush

METHOD

1 Preheat the oven to 180°C (350°F/Gas 4). Line the base and sides of a loaf tin with baking parchment. Sift the flour into a large bowl, add the butter, sugar, eggs, baking powder, spices, and marmalade, and mix until well combined.

2 Pour into the tin and smooth the top. Bake for 1 hour 15 minutes, or until risen and firm to the touch. Cover the top of the cake with foil for the last 30 minutes, if it starts to brown too quickly. Leave to cool in the tin for 5 minutes. Warm the marmalade in a pan, then brush the top of the cake generously with it. Remove from the tin, and leave to cool completely on a wire rack.

serves 8–10

prep 15 mins
• cook 1 hr
15 mins

18 x 9cm
(7 x 3$^{1}/_{2}$in) 2lb
loaf tin

freeze, before
adding the
topping, for
up to 3 months

Superfood loaf cake

Thanks to the seeds, this tasty cake has plenty of texture and is full of healthy ingredients, too.

INGREDIENTS

180ml (6^1/$_2$fl oz) sunflower oil
225g (8oz) light muscovado sugar
3 large eggs, separated
350g (12oz) raw beetroot,
    peeled and grated
juice of 1 lemon
75g (2^1/$_2$oz) sultanas
75g (2^1/$_2$oz) mixed seeds, or 20g (^{3}/$_4$oz) each
    linseeds, pumpkin, sunflower, and sesame seeds,
    plus extra for sprinkling
100g (3^1/$_2$oz) wholemeal self-raising flour
125g (4^1/$_2$oz) white self-raising flour
^{1}/$_2$ tsp bicarbonate of soda
1 tsp baking powder
^{1}/$_2$ tsp ground cinnamon

METHOD

1 Preheat the oven to 180°C (350°F/Gas 4). Grease the loaf tin and line with baking parchment.

2 Place the oil and sugar in a large bowl and beat until well combined. Add the egg yolks, one at a time, beating the mixture well between each addition. Stir in the grated beetroot, lemon juice, sultanas, and all but 2 tbsp of the seeds.

3 Sift the flours, bicarbonate of soda, baking powder, and cinnamon over the egg mixture and fold in thoroughly with a metal spoon.

4 Place the egg whites in a large clean, dry glass or metal bowl and whisk with a balloon whisk or an electric hand whisk until soft peaks form. Fold the beaten whites into the cake mixture.

5 Transfer the mixture to the prepared loaf tin and sprinkle with the reserved seeds. Bake for 1 hour and 15 minutes, or until a skewer inserted in the centre of the cake comes out clean. Remove from the oven and leave to cool in the tin for 10 minutes, then turn out and transfer to a wire rack to cool completely.

PREPARE AHEAD The cake keeps for 3–4 days in an airtight container.

serves 8

**prep 30 mins
• cook 1 hr
15 mins**

**900g (2lb)
loaf tin**

**freeze for
up to 3 months**

Stollen

This rich, fruity yeast bread is traditionally served at Christmas in Germany.

INGREDIENTS

200g (7oz) raisins
100g (3½oz) currants
100ml (3½fl oz) rum
400g (14oz) plain flour,
  plus extra for dusting
7g sachet easy-blend dried yeast
60g (2oz) caster sugar
100ml (3½fl oz) milk
few drops of pure vanilla extract

pinch of salt
½ tsp ground mixed spice
2 eggs
175g (6oz) unsalted butter, at
  room temperature
200g (7oz) mixed candied peel
100g (3½oz) ground almonds
icing sugar, for dusting

METHOD

1 Put the raisins and currants into a bowl, pour over the rum, and leave to soak overnight.

2 The following day, sift the flour into a large bowl, make a well in the centre, sprinkle in the yeast, and add 1 tsp of the sugar. Gently heat the milk until lukewarm, and pour on top of the yeast. Leave to stand at room temperature for 15 minutes, or until frothy.

3 Add the rest of the sugar, the vanilla extract, salt, mixed spice, eggs, and butter. Using a wooden spoon, or hand-mixer with a dough hook, mix, then knead the ingredients together for 5 minutes, or until they form a smooth dough.

4 Transfer to a lightly floured work surface. Add the candied peel, soaked raisins and currants, and ground almonds to the dough, kneading for a few minutes, or until evenly incorporated. Return the dough to the bowl, cover with cling film or a damp tea towel, and leave to rise in a warm place until it has doubled in size.

5 Preheat the oven to 160°C (325°F/Gas 3). Line a baking tray with baking parchment paper. On a floured surface, roll out the dough to make a 30 x 25cm (12 x 10in) rectangle. Fold one long side over, just beyond the middle, then fold over the other long side to overlap the first, curling it over slightly on top to create the stollen shape. Transfer to the baking tray, and put in a warm place to rise again, until doubled in size.

6 Bake in the oven for 50 minutes, or until risen and pale golden. Transfer to a wire rack to cool completely, then generously dust with icing sugar. Serve cut into thick slices, with or without butter.

GOOD WITH Other sweet festive treats, such as marzipan sweets, or mince pies.

makes 1 loaf

prep 35 mins,
plus soaking,
resting, and
rising
• cook 50 mins

soak the
raisins and
currants
overnight

freeze, before
dusting the
top, for up to
1 month

TRAYBAKES & SLICES

Double chocolate brownies

Proving that two types of chocolate are always better than one, these brownies are rich, moist, and toothsome.

INGREDIENTS
300g (10oz) 70 per cent dark chocolate, chopped
125g (4^1/$_2$oz) unsalted butter, at room temperature
200g (7oz) light soft brown sugar
75ml (2^1/$_2$fl oz) olive oil
3 medium eggs, beaten
1 tsp pure vanilla extract
75g (2^1/$_2$oz) plain flour
25g (scant 1oz) cocoa powder
^{1}/$_2$ tsp baking powder
175g (6oz) white chocolate, chopped

METHOD
1 Preheat the oven to 180°C (350°F/Gas 4) and grease the baking tin.

2 Place 200g (7oz) of the dark chocolate and the butter in a heatproof bowl, set it over a saucepan of simmering water, and stir occasionally until melted.

3 Place the butter and chocolate mixture, sugar, olive oil, eggs, and vanilla extract in a large bowl and mix until combined. Sift over the flour, cocoa powder, and baking powder, and fold in gently with a metal spoon. Then fold in the white chocolate and the remaining dark chocolate.

4 Transfer the mixture to the prepared tin and bake for 25–30 minutes, or until set on top and a skewer inserted into the centre comes out with some moist crumbs attached. Remove from the oven and leave to cool completely in the tin, then remove from the tin and cut into 16 pieces.

PREPARE AHEAD The brownies will keep for up to 5 days in an airtight container.

makes 16

prep 20 mins
• cook 30 mins

23cm (9in)
square cake
tin or
25 x 15cm
(10 x 6in)
cake tin

freeze for
up to 3 months

White chocolate and macadamia nut blondies

A white chocolate version of the ever-popular brownie.

INGREDIENTS

300g (10oz) white chocolate, chopped
175g (6oz) unsalted butter, cubed
300g (10oz) caster sugar
4 large eggs
225g (8oz) plain flour
100g (3½oz) macadamia nuts, roughly chopped

METHOD

1 Preheat the oven to 200°C (400°F/Gas 6). Line the base and sides of the tin with baking parchment. In a bowl set over a pan of simmering water, melt the chocolate and butter together, stirring now and again until smooth. Remove, and leave to cool for about 20 minutes.

2 Once the chocolate has melted, mix in the sugar (the mixture may well become thick and grainy, but the eggs will loosen the mixture). Using a balloon whisk, stir in the eggs one at a time, making sure each is well mixed in before you add the next. Sift in the flour, fold it in, and then stir in the nuts. Pour the mixture into the tin and gently spread it out into the corners. Bake for 20 minutes, or until just firm to the touch on top but still soft underneath. Leave to cool completely in the tin, then cut into 24 squares, or rectangles, for bigger blondies.

makes 24

**prep 25 mins
• cook 20 mins**

**22 x 30cm
(8¾ x 12in)
rectangular
cake tin**

Toffee brownies

These attractively decorated brownies would be perfect for a children's party.

INGREDIENTS

100g (3½oz) dark chocolate, broken into pieces, plus 50g (1¾oz) extra, to decorate
175g (6oz) unsalted butter
350g (12oz) caster sugar
4 large eggs
2 tsp pure vanilla extract
200g (7oz) plain flour
1 tsp baking powder
100g (3½oz) pecans, roughly chopped
200g (7oz) creamy toffees
75ml (2½fl oz) double cream

METHOD

1 Preheat the oven to 180°C (350°F/Gas 4). Line the base of the baking tray with baking parchment.

2 Place the chocolate in a large heatproof bowl with the butter. Set the bowl over a saucepan of simmering water and stir occasionally until the chocolate has melted and the butter is well combined. Remove from the heat, then stir the sugar into the melted chocolate mixture.

3 Lightly beat the eggs with the vanilla in another bowl, then stir them into the chocolate mixture. Sift the flour and baking powder into the mixture, fold in lightly with a metal spoon, then fold in the pecans.

4 Place the toffees and cream in a saucepan over a gentle heat and stir continuously until melted.

5 Transfer half the chocolate mixture to the baking tin and spoon ½ of the toffee sauce over. Spread the rest of the chocolate mixture on top and bake for 40–45 minutes, or until firm to the touch. Remove from the oven, leave to cool in the tin for 20 minutes, then turn out. Remove the baking parchment, then transfer to a wire rack to cool completely.

6 Decorate by reheating the remaining toffee sauce. Place the extra chocolate in a small heatproof bowl, set the bowl over a saucepan of simmering water, and stir until the chocolate has melted. Drizzle the toffee sauce over the brownie, followed by the melted chocolate, using the tip of a teaspoon. Leave to cool, then cut into 18 pieces.

PREPARE AHEAD The brownies will keep in an airtight container for up to 5 days.

makes 18

prep 30 mins
• cook 40–45
mins

28 x 18cm
(11 x 7in)
shallow
cake tin

freeze for
up to 3 months

Flapjacks

These chewy bars are simple to make, using only a few storecupboard ingredients.

INGREDIENTS

225g (8oz) unsalted butter, plus extra for greasing
225g (8oz) light soft brown sugar
2 tbsp golden syrup
350g (12oz) rolled oats

METHOD

1 Preheat the oven to 150°C (300°F/Gas 2). Lightly grease the square cake tin.

2 Put the butter, sugar, and syrup in a large saucepan, and heat over a medium-low heat until the butter has melted. Remove the pan from the heat, and stir in the oats.

3 Transfer the mixture to the prepared tin, and press down firmly. Bake for 40 minutes, or until evenly golden and just beginning to brown at the edges.

4 Leave to cool for 10 minutes, then cut into 16 squares, or 20 rectangles. Leave in the tin until completely cooled.

PREPARE AHEAD These will keep for a few days in an airtight container.

serves 16–20

prep 15 mins
• cook 40 mins

25cm (10in)
square cake tin

Sticky date flapjacks

These flapjacks with a gooey layer of dates are ideal for lunch boxes.

INGREDIENTS

200g (7oz) stoned dates (medjool are best), chopped
$\frac{1}{2}$ tsp bicarbonate of soda
200g (7oz) unsalted butter
200g (7oz) light soft brown sugar
2 tbsp golden syrup
300g (10oz) rolled oats

METHOD

1 Preheat the oven to 160°C (325°F/Gas 3). Line the square cake tin with baking parchment. Place the dates and bicarbonate of soda in a pan with enough water to cover, simmer for 5 minutes, then drain, reserving the liquid. Process to a purée in a blender with 3 tbsp cooking liquid, then set aside.

2 Melt the butter, sugar, and syrup together in a large pan, stirring until the mixture forms a smooth sauce (you might need to give it a quick whisk to bring it together). Stir in the oats, then press half the mixture into the base of the tin.

3 Spread the date purée over the top of the oats, then spoon the remaining oat mixture over the top, gently easing it over the dates. Bake for 40 minutes, or until golden brown. Leave to cool in the tin for 10 minutes, then mark into 16 squares. Leave to cool completely in the tin, before cutting and serving.

makes 16

**prep 25 mins
• cook 40 mins**

**20cm (8in)
square cake tin
• blender**

Sticky toffee shortbreads

Shortbread becomes utterly addictive once topped with rich chocolate and sticky toffee.

INGREDIENTS

250g (9oz) unsalted butter, at room temperature
175g (6oz) golden granulated sugar
225g (8oz) plain flour
125g (4^1/$_2$oz) semolina
4–5 tbsp ready-made toffee sauce
150g (5^1/$_2$oz) dark chocolate, broken into pieces
150g (5^1/$_2$oz) white chocolate, broken into pieces

METHOD

1 Preheat the oven to 150°C (300°F/Gas 2). Lightly grease the tin and line with baking parchment. To make the shortbread, whisk the butter and sugar together until pale and creamy, then add the flour and semolina, and mix until well combined. Press the mixture into the prepared tin, and level the surface with a knife.

2 Bake in the oven for 40–45 minutes, or until lightly golden, then remove and leave it to cool. Spoon the toffee sauce evenly over the shortbread, and smooth the surface with the back of a spoon until level.

3 In two separate heatproof bowls, each set over a pan of simmering water, melt the dark and white chocolate. Spoon blobs of dark and white chocolate randomly over the toffee sauce layer, and create a marbled effect by blending them slightly with the end of a teaspoon. Chill for a couple of hours for the chocolate to set. Remove from the tin, place on a chopping board, and cut into 24 small squares with a large knife.

makes 24

prep 20 mins, plus chilling • cook 45–50 mins

allow 2 hrs for chilling

20cm (8in) square shallow loose-bottomed cake tin

Mocha slices

A whisper of coffee flavour suffuses the rich topping on this shortbread slice. It makes a pleasing dessert.

INGREDIENTS

300g (10oz) all-butter shortbread biscuits
150g (5$\frac{1}{2}$oz) unsalted butter
100g (3$\frac{1}{2}$oz) dark chocolate,
   broken into small pieces
100g (3$\frac{1}{2}$oz) coffee-flavoured chocolate,
   broken into small pieces
3 large eggs
75g (2$\frac{1}{2}$oz) caster sugar
1 tbsp cocoa powder

METHOD

1 Preheat the oven to 190°C (375°F/Gas 5). Grease the tart tin and line with baking parchment.

2 Place the shortbread in a large plastic bag and seal. Hit the bag with the side of a rolling pin until the biscuits are crushed into crumbs. Melt half the butter in a medium-sized saucepan, then remove from the heat, and add the crushed biscuits. Stir well, until the crumbs are completely coated in the butter, then spread the mixture on to the base of the prepared tin, pressing it firmly into the edges of the tin. Set aside.

3 Melt the dark and coffee-flavoured chocolate with the remaining butter in a small heatproof bowl set over a pan of simmering water, stirring occasionally. Then remove the bowl and set aside to cool slightly.

4 Whisk together the eggs and sugar in a large bowl for about 5–8 minutes, until thick and creamy, then fold in the melted chocolate. Pour the mixture over the biscuit base. Bake for about 10–15 minutes, until the top forms a crust. Remove and leave to cool completely in the tin. Sprinkle with cocoa powder, and slice into 8 rectangular slices to serve.

GOOD WITH Pouring cream and fresh cherries or raspberries.

makes 8

prep 20 mins • cook 15–20 mins

20 x 30cm (8 x 12in) rectangular shallow loose-bottomed tart tin

Cherry flapjacks

These upmarket flapjacks have the perfect texture, and the oats give them a delicious toasty flavour.

INGREDIENTS

150g (5$^{1}/_{2}$oz) unsalted butter
75g (2$^{1}/_{2}$oz) light soft brown sugar
2 tbsp golden syrup
350g (12oz) rolled oats
125g (4$^{1}/_{2}$oz) glacé cherries, quartered, or
   75g (2$^{1}/_{2}$oz) dried cherries, roughly chopped
50g (1$^{3}/_{4}$oz) raisins
100g (3$^{1}/_{2}$oz) milk or white chocolate,
  broken into small pieces, to decorate

METHOD

1 Preheat the oven to 180°C (350°F/Gas 4). Lightly grease the cake tin.

2 Place the butter, sugar, and syrup in a medium saucepan over a low heat, and stir until the butter and sugar have melted. Remove the saucepan from the heat, add the oats, cherries, and raisins, and stir until well mixed. Transfer the mixture to the prepared tin and press down.

3 Bake at the top of the oven for 25 minutes. Remove from the oven, allow to cool slightly in the tin, then mark into 18 pieces with a knife.

4 When the block of flapjacks is cold, place the chocolate in a small heatproof bowl, set it over a saucepan of simmering water, and stir occasionally until the chocolate has melted. Drizzle the melted chocolate over the flapjacks using a teaspoon, then chill for about 10 minutes, or until the chocolate has set.

5 Remove the block of flapjacks from the tin and cut into pieces as marked.

PREPARE AHEAD The flapjacks can be kept in an airtight container for up to 1 week.

makes 18

prep 20 mins,
plus chilling
• cook 25 mins

20cm (8in)
square shallow
cake tin

Florentine slices

Cut into slices, these yummy treats are an easy-to-make great variation on traditional round Florentines.

INGREDIENTS
225g (8oz) plain chocolate, broken into pieces
60g (2oz) unsalted butter
115g (4oz) demerara sugar
1 egg, beaten
60g (2oz) mixed dried fruit
115g (4oz) desiccated coconut
60g (2oz) chopped mixed peel or glacé cherries

METHOD
1 Grease the cake tin and line with baking parchment.

2 Place the chocolate in a small heatproof bowl, set it over a saucepan of simmering water, and stir occasionally until the chocolate has melted. Spoon the melted chocolate into the prepared cake tin, and spread it evenly over the base. Chill in the refrigerator to set while you make the Florentine mixture.

3 Preheat the oven to 150°C (300°F/Gas 2). Place the butter and sugar in a large bowl and cream together until light and fluffy. Beat in the egg.

4 Mix the remaining ingredients in a separate bowl, then add them to the butter mixture. Stir well to ensure the fruit is evenly distributed, then spoon the mixture over the set chocolate in the tin.

5 Bake in the centre of the oven for 40–45 minutes, or until golden brown. Remove from the oven and leave to stand in the tin for 5 minutes.

6 Mark out 16 squares using a sharp knife, but make sure you do not cut into the chocolate – it is still runny and if your knife touches it, the sides of the squares will be smeared with chocolate. Leave until completely cold, then cut right through, loosen each square with a knife, and remove carefully from the tin.

PREPARE AHEAD The slices can be stored in an airtight container for up to 1 week.

makes 16

**prep 20 mins
• cook 40–45 mins**

**20cm (8in)
square cake tin**

Panforte

This famous cake from Siena, Italy, dates from the 13th century.

INGREDIENTS

rice paper, for lining
115g (4oz) whole blanched almonds,
   toasted and roughly chopped
125g (4$^{1}/_{2}$oz) hazelnuts,
   toasted and roughly chopped
200g (7oz) mixed candied orange and
   lemon peel, chopped
115g (4oz) dried figs, roughly chopped
finely grated zest of 1 lemon
$^{1}/_{2}$ tsp ground cinnamon
$^{1}/_{2}$ tsp freshly grated nutmeg
$^{1}/_{4}$ tsp ground cloves
$^{1}/_{4}$ tsp ground allspice
75g (2$^{1}/_{2}$oz) rice flour or plain flour
30g (1oz) unsalted butter
140g (5oz) caster sugar
4 tbsp clear honey
icing sugar, to dust

METHOD

1 Line the base and sides of the cake tin with greaseproof paper, then put a disc of rice paper on top of the paper. Preheat the oven to 180°C (350°F/Gas 4).

2 Put the almonds, hazelnuts, candied peel, figs, lemon zest, cinnamon, nutmeg, cloves, allspice, and flour in a large bowl, and mix well.

3 Put the butter, caster sugar, and honey in a pan, and heat gently until melted. Pour into the fruit and nut mixture, and stir to combine. Spoon into the prepared tin and, with damp hands, press down to create a smooth, even layer.

4 Bake for 30 minutes, then remove from the oven, leaving it in the tin to cool and become firm. When completely cold, remove the panforte from the tin. Peel off the paper, but leave the rice paper stuck to the bottom of the cake.

5 Dust heavily with icing sugar, and serve cut into small wedges.

PREPARE AHEAD This can be stored in an airtight container for up to three days.

serves 12–16

prep 30 mins
• cook 30 mins

20cm (8in)
loose-
bottomed
cake tin

Apricot crumble shortbread

This is a fruity twist on plain shortbread with a sweet, textured topping.

INGREDIENTS

200g (7oz) unsalted butter,
   at room temperature
100g (3^1/$_2$oz) caster sugar
200g (7oz) plain flour
100g (3^1/$_2$oz) cornflour
400g can apricots in natural juice,
   drained and roughly chopped

For the topping

75g (2^1/$_2$oz) butter, diced
150g (5^1/$_2$oz) plain flour
75g (2^1/$_2$oz) demerara sugar
   or caster sugar

METHOD

1 Line the cake tin with baking parchment. Cream the butter and sugar together in a bowl until pale and creamy. Sift in the flour and cornflour and combine so that the mixture comes together to form a dough. (You will probably need to use your hands to bring it together at the end.) Knead the dough lightly until smooth, then push evenly into the base of the tin and smooth the top. Chill in the refrigerator for at least an hour, or until firm.

2 Preheat the oven to 180°C (350°F/Gas 4). Make the topping by rubbing the butter into the flour in a bowl with your fingertips, until the mixture resembles breadcrumbs. Stir in the sugar. Scatter the apricots evenly over the chilled base, then top with the buttery crumb mixture, pressing down quite firmly. Bake for 45 minutes, or until a skewer inserted into the centre comes out clean with no uncooked mixture on it (it might be a bit damp from the fruit, though). Leave to cool in the tin. When cold, remove from the tin, and cut into 10 bars or 20 squares.

**makes 10 bars,
or 20 squares**

**prep 20 mins,
plus chilling
• cook
45 mins**

**12.5 x 35.5cm
(5¼ x 14¼in)
rectangular
cake tin**

Raspberry, lemon, and almond bake

Sweet almond cake topped with tart raspberries is a moreish treat.

INGREDIENTS

125g (4¹/₂oz) plain flour
1 tsp baking powder
75g (2¹/₂oz) ground almonds
150g (5¹/₂oz) unsalted butter, cubed
200g (7oz) caster sugar
juice of 1 lemon (about 3 tbsp)
1 tsp pure vanilla extract
2 large eggs
200g (7oz) fresh raspberries
icing sugar, to dust (optional)

METHOD

1 Preheat the oven to 180°C (350°F/Gas 4). Line the base and sides of the cake tin with baking parchment. Sift the flour into a bowl, add the baking powder and ground almonds, and mix well. In a pan, melt the butter, sugar, and lemon juice together, stirring until well combined.

2 Stir this syrupy mixture into the dry ingredients, then mix in the vanilla extract and the eggs, one at a time, until the mixture is smooth and well combined. Pour into the tin, then scatter the raspberries over the top. Bake for 35–40 minutes, or until golden, and a skewer inserted into the cake comes out clean.

3 Cool in the tin for 10 minutes, then turn out and cool completely on a wire rack. Dust with icing sugar before serving (if using). To serve, cut into rectangles.

serves 8

**prep 20 mins
• cook 35–40
mins**

**20cm (8in)
square
loose-
bottomed
cake tin**

**freeze for
up to 2 months**

Toffee apple traybake

Bake this on a winter evening and serve warm for a special treat.

INGREDIENTS

350g (12oz) Bramley apples, peeled,
 cored, and thinly sliced
squeeze of lemon juice
350g (12oz) self-raising flour
2 tsp baking powder
350g (12oz) light soft brown sugar
4 large eggs, lightly beaten
225g (8oz) unsalted butter, melted
1 tbsp caster sugar

For the toffee sauce

100g (3^1/$_2$oz) unsalted butter
100g (3^1/$_2$oz) light soft brown sugar
1 tbsp lemon juice
salt

METHOD

1 Preheat the oven to 180°C (350°F/Gas 4). Line the base and sides of the tin with baking parchment. Put the apple slices in a bowl, and toss with the lemon juice to stop them turning brown while you make the cake mixture.

2 Sift the flour into a large mixing bowl, add the baking powder and brown sugar, and stir well. Mix in the eggs and the melted butter to make a smooth batter. Pour into the tin and smooth the top. Arrange the apple slices in three or four long lines along the top of the mixture, and sprinkle with the caster sugar. Bake for 45 minutes, or until the cake is firm to the touch, and a skewer inserted into the middle comes out clean.

3 Meanwhile, make the sauce by melting the butter, sugar, and lemon juice in a pan with a pinch of salt, whisking with a balloon whisk or electric hand whisk until the mixture is thick, melted, and smooth. Leave to cool slightly. Pour the sauce over the cake while it is still in the tin, gently brushing the sauce all over the top of the cake. Serve warm or cold.

GOOD WITH A spoonful of crème fraîche.

**makes 18
squares**

**prep 20 mins
• cook 45 mins**

**22 x 30cm
(8¾ x 12in)
rectangular
cake tin**

White chocolate cakes

These delicious cakes are studded with crunchy walnuts.

INGREDIENTS

50g (1³/₄oz) unsalted butter, at room temperature
50g (1³/₄oz) caster sugar
1 tsp pure vanilla extract
2 medium eggs, lightly beaten
100g (3¹/₂oz) self-raising flour
200g (7oz) white chocolate, finely chopped
100g (3¹/₂oz) walnuts, chopped

For the topping

200g (7oz) white chocolate
50g (1³/₄oz) walnuts, chopped, to decorate

METHOD

1 Preheat the oven to 160°C (325°F/Gas 3). Grease the deep square tin with butter. Line with baking parchment and set it aside.

2 Cream the butter, sugar, and vanilla extract in a bowl with a wooden spoon or an electric hand whisk until pale and creamy. Add the eggs a little at a time, beating well after each addition. Gently fold in the flour, then the chocolate and the chopped walnuts.

3 Spread the mixture in the tin and smooth the top. Bake for 30–35 minutes, or until set. Cool in the tin for 10 minutes before turning out on to a wire rack to cool.

4 For the topping, melt the white chocolate in a heatproof bowl placed over gently simmering water, stirring, until smooth and glossy. Spread it evenly over the cooled cake. Allow it to set, then decorate with chopped walnuts, and cut it into 9 squares.

makes 9

prep 10 mins
• cook 30–35 mins

16cm (7in)
deep square
cake tin

Chocolate biscuit cake

Crunchy, chocolatey, and sweet, this no-bake cake couldn't be easier to make.

INGREDIENTS

150g (5^1/$_2$oz) unsalted butter
250g (9oz) dark chocolate, broken into pieces
2 tbsp golden syrup
450g (1lb) digestive biscuits, crushed
handful of plump golden raisins
handful of unskinned almonds, roughly chopped

METHOD

1 Lightly grease the square tin. In a small pan, melt the butter, chocolate, and syrup, then remove from the heat and stir in the biscuits, raisins, and almonds. Mix well, then press the mixture into the tin with the back of a spoon. Transfer to the refrigerator to cool completely and solidify for at least 2 hours.

2 Turn out the cake from its tin, and slice to serve.

serves 6

prep 10 mins

**allow at least
2 hrs for
chilling**

**18cm (7in)
deep square
cake tin**

Madeleines

These little treats were made famous by the writer, Marcel Proust.

INGREDIENTS

60g (2oz) unsalted butter, melted but not hot,
    plus extra for greasing
60g (2oz) caster sugar
2 eggs
1 tsp pure vanilla extract
60g (2oz) self-raising flour, sifted
icing sugar, to dust

METHOD

1 Preheat the oven to 180°C (350°F/Gas 4). Carefully brush the moulds with melted butter and dust with flour.

2 Put the sugar, eggs, and vanilla extract into a mixing bowl and whisk until the mixture is pale, thick, and will hold a trail. This should take 5 minutes with an electric whisk, or slightly longer if you are using a balloon whisk.

3 Sift the flour over the top, and pour the melted butter down the side of the mixture. Using a large metal spoon, fold them in carefully and quickly, being careful not to knock out any air.

4 Fill the moulds with the mixture, and bake in the oven for 10 minutes. Remove from the oven, and transfer to a wire rack to cool, before dusting with icing sugar.

makes 12

prep
15–20 mins
• cook 10 mins

madeleine tin
or 12-hole
bun tin

freeze for
up to 1 month

French almond financiers

So-called because these cakes are said to resemble gold bars.

INGREDIENTS

60g (2oz) ground almonds
85g (3oz) icing sugar, sifted
30g (1oz) plain flour, plus extra for dusting
pinch of salt
85g (3oz) unsalted butter,
    plus extra for greasing
3 egg whites
$\frac{1}{2}$ tsp pure vanilla extract

METHOD

1 Preheat the oven to 200°C (400°F/Gas 6). Grease the moulds or cake tin holes well with butter, and dust with flour.

2 Mix the almonds, icing sugar, flour, and salt together. Melt the butter, but do not let it get too hot. In a separate, clean, dry glass or metal bowl, whisk the egg whites until frothy, but not too thick. Add to the almond mixture with the butter and vanilla extract, and fold in.

3 Half-fill the greased moulds, and bake in the centre of the oven for 10–12 minutes, or until they have risen a little, and are golden and springy to the touch. Allow to cool in the moulds for 5 minutes, then carefully remove and allow to cool completely on a wire rack.

makes 12

**prep 15 mins
• cook 10–12
mins**

**12 financier
or barquette
moulds, or
a 12-hole
cake tin**

**freeze for
up to 3 months**

Nutty "drop" buns

These traditional-style buns are great for the lunchbox or as an after-school treat.

INGREDIENTS
175g (6oz) self-raising flour
60g (2oz) semolina or ground rice
115g (4oz) unsalted butter, cut in small pieces
85g (3oz) golden granulated sugar
115g (4oz) dates, pitted and finely chopped
60g (2oz) walnuts, chopped
2 large eggs, beaten
1 tsp pure vanilla extract
12 walnut halves, to decorate

For the icing
1 tbsp instant coffee granules
115g (4oz) golden icing sugar

METHOD
1 Preheat the oven to 190°C (375°F/Gas 5) and grease the bun tray. Place the flour and semolina or ground rice in a large bowl, then add the butter and rub in with your fingertips. Stir in the sugar, dates, and walnuts. Add the eggs and vanilla extract, and mix to a stiff consistency.

2 Spoon the mixture into the bun tray and bake towards the top of the oven for approximately 10–12 minutes. Remove from the oven and leave to cool slightly in the tin before turning out on a wire rack to cool.

3 Make the icing by mixing the instant coffee granules with 1 tbsp boiling water. Blend the coffee solution with the icing sugar until the icing is of a dropping consistency.

4 Drizzle the icing over each bun using a teaspoon, then top with half a walnut, and leave the icing to set.

makes 12

prep 15 mins
• cook 12 mins

eat on the day
of making

12-cup
non-stick
bun tray

Fondant fancies

Gorgeous to look at and gorgeous to eat, these are perfect party cakes.

INGREDIENTS
175g (6oz) unsalted butter,
  at room temperature
175g (6oz) caster sugar
3 large eggs
1 tsp pure vanilla extract
175g (6oz) self-raising flour
2 tbsp milk
2–3 tbsp raspberry or red cherry conserve
icing flowers, to decorate (optional)

For the buttercream
75g (2^1/$_2$oz) unsalted butter, at
  room temperature
150g (5^1/$_2$oz) icing sugar

For the icing
juice of ^{1}/$_2$ lemon
450g (1lb) icing sugar
1–2 drops natural pink food colouring

METHOD
1 Preheat the oven to 190°C (375°F/Gas 5). Grease the cake tin and line with baking parchment. Place the butter and sugar in a large bowl and beat until pale and fluffy. Set aside.

2 Lightly beat the eggs and vanilla extract in another large bowl. Add about ^{1}/$_4$ of the egg mixture and 1 tbsp of the flour to the butter mixture and beat well, then add the rest of the egg, a little at a time, beating as you go. Sift over the rest of the flour, add the milk, and fold in with a metal spoon.

3 Transfer the mixture to the prepared cake tin and bake on the middle shelf of the oven for about 25 minutes, or until lightly golden and springy to the touch. Remove from the oven, leave to cool in the tin for about 10 minutes, then remove from the tin and cool upside down on a wire rack.

4 To make the buttercream, beat the butter with the icing sugar until the mixture is smooth. Set aside.

5 Slice the cake horizontally and spread the fruit conserve on one half and the buttercream on the other. Sandwich together, then cut into 16 equal squares.

6 To make the icing, put the lemon juice in a measuring jug and fill it up to 60ml (2fl oz) with hot water. Mix this with the icing sugar, stirring continuously and adding more hot water as required until the mixture is smooth. Add 1–2 drops pink food colouring and stir well.

7 Use a palette knife to transfer the cakes to a wire rack placed over a board or plate (to catch the drips), then drizzle with the icing to cover the cakes completely, or just cover the tops of the cakes and allow the icing to drip down the sides so the sponge layers are visible.

8 Decorate with icing flowers (if using), then leave to set for about 15 minutes. Use a clean palette knife to transfer each cake carefully to a paper case.

PREPARE AHEAD Store the iced fondants on a tray, covered, in the refrigerator for up to 1 day.

makes 16

prep 30 mins
• cook 25 mins

20cm (8in)
square cake tin
• paper cases

freeze, unfilled
and without
icing, for up to
3 months

Berry friands

Friands are small French-style cakes flavoured with almonds.

INGREDIENTS

100g (3$^1/_2$oz) icing sugar

45g (1$^1/_2$oz) plain flour

75g (2$^1/_2$oz) ground almonds

3 large egg whites

75g (2$^1/_2$oz) unsalted butter, melted

150g (5$^1/_2$oz) mixed fresh berries,
    such as blueberries and raspberries

METHOD

1 Preheat the oven to 180°C (350°F/Gas 4). Line a muffin tin with 6 muffin cases. Sift the icing sugar and flour into a bowl, then stir in the ground almonds. In a separate clean, dry glass or metal bowl, whisk the egg whites until they form soft peaks.

2 Gently fold the flour mixture and the melted butter into the egg whites, to make a smooth batter. Spoon the batter into the muffin cases, then scatter the berries over, pressing them down slightly into the batter so they all fit in. Bake for 30–35 minutes, or until golden brown and risen. Leave to cool in the tin.

makes 6

prep 15 mins
• cook 30–35 mins

6-cup
muffin tin
• muffin cases

Lemon poppy seed muffins

These muffins are delightful served with brunch or as a teatime treat.

INGREDIENTS
400g (14oz) plain white flour
$1/2$ tsp baking powder
$1/2$ tsp baking soda
$1/4$ tsp salt
100g ($3^1/_2$oz) caster sugar
$2^1/_2$ tbsp poppy seeds, black or white
finely grated zest of 2 large lemons
2 eggs
250ml (9fl oz) soured cream
60g (2oz) unsalted butter, melted and cooled
4 tbsp sunflower oil
icing sugar, for dusting

METHOD
1 Preheat the oven to 200°C (400°F/Gas 6). Line a 12-hole muffin tin with 12 muffin cases and set aside. Sift the flour, baking powder, baking soda, and salt into a bowl. Stir in the sugar, poppy seeds, and lemon zest, then make a well in the centre of the dry ingredients.

2 In a separate bowl, beat the eggs. Mix in the soured cream, butter, and oil and pour the mixture into the centre of the dry ingredients. Mix together lightly to make a lumpy batter. Spoon the mixture into the paper cases, filling each case $3/4$ full.

3 Bake the muffins for 20 minutes, or until well risen, and a skewer inserted in to the centre comes out clean. Sift icing sugar over the tops while still warm.

makes 12

prep 10 mins
• cook 20 mins

12-cup muffin tin
• muffin cases

Banana and chocolate chip muffins

These nice moist muffins have a good banana flavour and plenty of oozing chocolate.

INGREDIENTS

100g (3½oz) plain flour
45g (1½oz) fine cornmeal
1 tsp baking powder
1 tsp bicarbonate of soda
100g (3½oz) golden caster sugar
45g (1½oz) unsalted butter, melted
1 medium egg, beaten
2 bananas, peeled and well mashed
90ml (3fl oz) buttermilk, or 85g (3oz) plain yogurt
50g (1¾oz) milk chocolate, chopped into small chunks

METHOD

1 Preheat the oven to 200°C (400°F/Gas 6). Line a muffin tin with 8 muffin cases.

2 Sift together the flour, cornmeal, baking powder, and bicarbonate of soda in a large bowl. Stir in the sugar, then set aside.

3 Place the melted butter, beaten egg, mashed bananas, and buttermilk or yogurt in a separate bowl and mix together. Fold the banana mixture gently into the flour mixture using a metal spoon, taking care not to overmix. Fold in the chocolate chunks.

4 Spoon the mixture into the muffin cases, and bake for 20–30 minutes, or until golden brown and firm to the touch. Remove from the oven and leave to cool completely in the tin.

PREPARE AHEAD The muffins keep for up to 1 week in an airtight tin.

makes 8

prep 15 mins
• cook 30 mins

standard
muffin tin
• muffin cases

freeze for
up to 3 months

Apple muffins

These are lovely served straight from the oven for breakfast.

INGREDIENTS

1 Golden Delicious apple,
    peeled and chopped
2 tsp lemon juice
115g (4oz) light demerara sugar,
    plus extra for sprinkling
200g (7oz) plain flour
85g (3oz) wholemeal flour
4 tsp baking powder
1 tbsp ground mixed spice
½ tsp salt
60g (2oz) pecan nuts, chopped
250ml (9fl oz) milk
4 tbsp sunflower oil
1 egg, beaten

METHOD

1 Preheat the oven to 200°C (400°F/Gas 6). Line a 12-hole muffin tin with 12 muffin cases and set aside. Put the apple in a bowl, add the lemon juice, and toss. Add 4 tbsp of the sugar and set aside for 5 minutes.

2 Meanwhile, sift the plain and wholemeal flours, baking powder, mixed spice, and salt into a large bowl, tipping in any bran left in the sieve. Stir in the remaining sugar and pecans, then make a well in the centre of the dry ingredients.

3 Beat together the milk, oil, and egg, then add the apple. Tip the wet ingredients into the centre of the dry ingredients, and mix together lightly to make a lumpy batter.

4 Spoon the mixture into the paper cases, filling each case ¾ full. Bake the muffins for 20–25 minutes, or until the tops are peaked and brown. Transfer the muffins to a wire rack and sprinkle with extra sugar. Eat warm or cooled.

makes 12

prep 10 mins
• cook 20–25 mins

12-cup muffin tin
• muffin cases

Blueberry muffins

An ever-popular flavour for muffins; this version has a hint of lemon.

INGREDIENTS

50g (1³/₄oz) unsalted butter
250g (9oz) self-raising flour
1 tsp baking powder
75g (2¹/₂oz) caster sugar
finely grated zest of 1 lemon (optional)
salt
250g (9oz) plain yogurt
2 large eggs, lightly beaten
250g (9oz) blueberries

METHOD

1 Preheat the oven to 200°C (400°F/Gas 6). Line a muffin tin with 12 muffin cases. Melt the butter in a small pan, then leave to cool. Sift the flour into a large bowl, mix in the baking powder, sugar, lemon zest (if using), and a pinch of salt, then make a well in the centre of the dry ingredients.

2 Mix the yogurt, eggs, and cooled melted butter together in a large jug, then pour into the dry ingredients, along with the blueberries. Mix lightly to make a lumpy batter – don't over-mix, or the muffins will be heavy.

3 Spoon evenly into the muffin cases and bake for 20 minutes, or until risen and golden. Cool in the tin for 5 minutes, then serve warm or leave to cool.

makes 12

**prep 15 mins
• cook 20 mins**

**12-cup
muffin tin
• muffin cases**

Chocolate muffins

Buttermilk makes these muffins really light.

INGREDIENTS
225g (8oz) plain flour
60g (2oz) cocoa powder
1 tbsp baking powder
pinch of salt
115g (4oz) light soft brown sugar
150g (5$\frac{1}{2}$oz) chocolate chips
250ml (9fl oz) buttermilk
6 tbsp sunflower oil
$\frac{1}{2}$ tsp pure vanilla extract
2 eggs

METHOD
1 Preheat the oven to 200°C (400°F/Gas 6). Line a 12-hole muffin tin with 12 muffin cases, and set aside.

2 Sift the flour, cocoa powder, baking powder, and salt into a large bowl. Stir in the sugar and chocolate chips, then make a well in the centre of the dry ingredients.

3 Beat together the buttermilk, oil, vanilla, and eggs and pour the mixture into the centre of the dry ingredients. Mix together lightly to make a lumpy batter. Spoon the mixture into the paper cases, filling each $^3/_4$ full.

4 Bake for 15 minutes, or until well risen and firm to the touch. Immediately transfer the muffins to a wire rack and leave to cool.

makes 12

prep 10 mins
• cook 15 mins

12-cup muffin tin
• muffin cases

Vanilla cupcakes

Coloured buttercream icing and small decorations transform these simple cupcakes into firm family favourites.

INGREDIENTS

225g (8oz) unsalted butter, at room temperature
225g (8oz) caster sugar
225g (8oz) self-raising flour
1 tsp baking powder
4 eggs
1 tsp pure vanilla extract
buttercream icing (see page 18),
   coloured pale pink and yellow
pink metallic balls, to decorate (optional)

METHOD

1 Preheat the oven to 180°C (350°F/Gas 4). Line a bun tray with 18–20 cupcake cases.

2 Place the butter, sugar, flour, baking powder, eggs, and vanilla extract in a large mixing bowl and beat until well combined. Spoon into the cupcake cases and bake for 18 minutes, or until risen and golden brown. Transfer to a wire rack to cool completely.

3 Pipe a swirl of either pink or yellow icing on top of each cupcake (see page 16), and add a few metallic balls.

makes 18–20

prep 15 mins
• cook 18 mins

standard bun tray
• standard
cupcake cases
• piping bag

Chocolate-frosted cupcakes

Kids will adore the creamy, chocolatey icing on these dainty cakes.

INGREDIENTS

125g (4¹/₂oz) unsalted butter,
    at room temperature
125g (4¹/₂oz) caster sugar
2 large eggs, beaten
125g (4¹/₂oz) self-raising flour, sifted
1 tsp pure vanilla extract
1 tbsp milk, if necessary

For the icing

100g (3¹/₂oz) icing sugar
15g (¹/₂oz) cocoa powder
100g (3¹/₂oz) unsalted butter, softened
few drops of pure vanilla extract
25g (scant 1oz) milk chocolate or dark chocolate,
    shaved with a vegetable peeler

METHOD

1 Preheat the oven to 190°C (375°F/Gas 5). Line the muffin tin with 12 muffin cases. Place the butter and sugar in a bowl, and cream until pale and fluffy. Beat in the eggs a little at a time, adding a little of the flour each time. Add the vanilla extract, then the rest of the flour, and mix until smooth and combined – the mixture should drop easily off a wooden spoon or whisk beaters. If it doesn't, stir in the milk.

2 Divide the mixture between the muffin cases using two teaspoons. Bake for 20 minutes, or until risen, golden, and firm to the touch. Transfer the cupcakes to a wire rack to cool.

3 To make the icing, sift the icing sugar and cocoa powder into a bowl, add the butter and the vanilla extract, and whisk with an electric hand whisk until the mixture is light and fluffy. Spread the icing over the cupcakes, giving the top of each one a swirly design. Scatter the chocolate shavings over.

makes 12

prep 25 mins
• cook 20 mins

12-cup
muffin tin
• muffin cases

freeze, before
icing, for up to
3 months

Orange and lemon cupcakes

These dainty, pretty cakes would be ideal for a girly tea party or a children's birthday party.

INGREDIENTS
200g (7oz) unsalted butter, at room temperature
200g (7oz) caster sugar
3 large eggs
200g (7oz) self-raising flour
finely grated zest and juice of 1 large orange
finely grated zest of 1 lemon
sugar sprinkles, to decorate

For the icing
50g (1³/₄oz) unsalted butter
125g (4¹/₂oz) icing sugar
juice of 1 lemon
few drops of natural yellow food colouring (optional)
few drops of natural orange food colouring (optional)

METHOD
1 Preheat the oven to 180°C (350°F/Gas 4). Line the muffin tin with 12 muffin cases.

2 Place the butter, sugar, eggs, flour, and orange and lemon zest in a bowl and beat until the mixture is pale and fluffy. Add the orange juice, a little at a time, until the mixture is of a dropping consistency.

3 Spoon the mixture into the muffin cases and bake for 25–30 minutes, or until lightly golden brown, risen, and springy to the touch. Remove from the oven and leave to cool in the tin for a few minutes before transferring to a wire rack to cool completely.

4 To make the icing, beat the butter and icing sugar together in a small bowl, then stir in the lemon juice. If using colouring, divide the icing mixture between two bowls. Mix a few drops of yellow colouring into one portion of icing, until you have the desired colour, and a few drops of orange into the other portion.

5 Spread the icing generously over the cakes then decorate with sugar sprinkles.

PREPARE AHEAD The cupcakes can be stored in an airtight container for several days.

makes 12

prep 15 mins
• cook 30 mins

12-cup
muffin tin
• muffin cases

freeze, without
the icing, for
up to 3 months

Chocolate cupcakes

Children will enjoy decorating these – they can add their favourite sweets to the simple chocolate topping.

INGREDIENTS

225g (8oz) unsalted butter,
   at room temperature
225g (8oz) caster sugar
225g (8oz) self-raising flour
1 tsp baking powder
4 eggs
2 tbsp cocoa powder
100g (3^1/$_2$oz) chocolate chips
175g (6oz) dark chocolate
flaked chocolate, to decorate

METHOD

1 Preheat the oven to 180°C (350°F/Gas 4). Line a bun tray with 18–20 cupcake cases.

2 Place the butter, caster sugar, flour, baking powder, eggs, and cocoa powder in a large mixing bowl, and beat until well combined. Stir in the chocolate chips, spoon the mixture into the cupcake cases, and bake for 18 minutes, or until well risen. Transfer to a wire rack to cool.

3 Melt the chocolate in a heatproof bowl over a pan of simmering water, then spoon over the top of the cooled cupcakes. Decorate with flaked chocolate. Leave until the chocolate has set.

makes 18–20

prep 15 mins
• cook 18 mins

standard bun tray
• standard
cupcake cases

Raspberry cupcakes

Elegant cakes that are perfect with after dinner coffee.

INGREDIENTS

225g (8oz) unsalted butter, at room temperature
225g (8oz) caster sugar
225g (8oz) self-raising flour
1 tsp baking powder
4 eggs
3 tbsp ground almonds
150g ($5^{1}/_{2}$oz) raspberries,
   plus 18–20 extra, to decorate
175g (6oz) white chocolate,
   plus extra, grated, to decorate

METHOD

1 Preheat the oven to 180°C (350°F/Gas 4). Line a bun tray with 18–20 cupcake cases.

2 Place the butter, caster sugar, flour, baking powder, and eggs in a large mixing bowl and beat until well combined. Stir in the almonds and raspberries, then spoon the mixture into the paper baking cases and bake for 18 minutes, or until risen and golden brown. Place on a wire rack to cool completely.

3 Put the white chocolate in a heatproof bowl, and melt it over a pan of barely simmering water, stirring occasionally until the chocolate is melted and smooth. Drizzle the chocolate over the top of the cupcakes. Decorate each one with grated white chocolate, and a raspberry.

makes 18–20

prep 15 mins
• cook 18 mins

standard bun tray
• standard
cupcake cases
• piping bag

Cinnamon apple and sultana cupcakes

Apples and sultanas are an infallible combination and seem made for each other in these delicious, moist cupcakes.

INGREDIENTS

115g (4oz) butter, at room temperature
115g (4oz) caster sugar
2 eggs
115g (4oz) self-raising flour
1/2 tsp baking powder
2 tsp ground cinnamon
3 green eating apples, peeled
   and grated, discarding cores
55g (2oz) sultanas

For the icing

225g (8oz) unsalted butter, at room temperature
450g (1lb) icing sugar, sifted
2 tbsp lemon juice
ground cinnamon, to dust

METHOD

1 Preheat the oven to 180°C (350°F/Gas 4). Line the muffin tray with 12 muffin cases.

2 Put the butter, sugar, eggs, flour, baking powder, and cinnamon in a large mixing bowl and beat well until light and fluffy. Add the grated apples and sultanas and beat briefly again.

3 Spoon the mixture into the muffin cases, and bake for about 15 minutes, or until well risen, golden, and the centres spring back when lightly pressed. Transfer to a wire rack to cool.

4 To make the icing, beat the softened unsalted butter in a bowl. Gradually beat in the icing sugar and lemon juice until soft and fluffy. Pipe or spoon the icing on top of the cupcakes and dust with cinnamon.

makes 12

prep 15 mins
• cook 15 mins

12-cup
muffin tin
• muffin cases

Lime drizzle cupcakes

These are equally delicious made with a large lemon instead of the limes.

INGREDIENTS
115g (4oz) unsalted butter, at room temperature
115g (4oz) caster sugar
2 eggs
finely grated zest of 1 lime
115g (4oz) self-raising flour
$1/2$ tsp baking powder

For the topping
finely grated zest of 1 lime, or
   zest of 1 lime with $3/4$ finely grated, and $1/4$ thinly pared
   and cut into thin strips, to decorate (optional)
juice of 2 limes
55g (2oz) caster sugar

METHOD
1 Preheat the oven to 180°C (350°F/Gas 4). Line the bun tray with 12 cupcake cases. Put the butter, sugar, eggs, flour, baking powder, and lime zest in a large mixing bowl. Beat well until light and fluffy.

2 Spoon the mixture into the cupcake cases, and bake for about 15 minutes, or until well risen and the centres spring back when lightly pressed. Transfer to a wire rack to cool.

3 Meanwhile, boil the strips of lime zest in water for 2 minutes (if using), drain, rinse with cold water, drain again, and set side.

4 Mix the lime juice, grated zest, and sugar together. Prick the tops of the cakes lightly with a skewer and spoon a little of the mixture over each cake, catching any surplus syrup in a bowl underneath to drizzle again. Leave to set for a few seconds then repeat until all the drizzle is used. Decorate by coating the strips of lime zest (if using) with caster sugar and use to top each cupcake. Leave to cool. The lime juice will sink in leaving a lovely crusty top.

makes 12

prep 15 mins
• cook 15 mins

**12-cup
standard
bun tray
• standard
cupcake cases**

Strawberry and cream cupcakes

These cupcakes are filled with a fresh strawberry filling and are a luscious treat for afternoon tea or pretty enough for a dessert.

INGREDIENTS

2 eggs, separated
115g (4oz) caster sugar
85g (3oz) unsalted butter, at room temperature
85g (3oz) self-raising flour
30g (1oz) cornflour
$^{1}/_{4}$ tsp pure vanilla extract

For the filling and topping

225g (8oz) strawberries
30g (1oz) caster sugar
A few drops of lemon juice
150ml (5fl oz) double or whipping cream

METHOD

1 Preheat the oven to 200°C (400°F/Gas 6). Line the bun tray with 12 cupcake cases.

2 Place the egg whites in a clean, dry glass or metal bowl and whisk until stiff, then whisk in 1 tbsp of the sugar and set aside. In another bowl, beat the butter and sugar with an electric hand whisk or wooden spoon until light and fluffy. Beat in the egg yolks. Sift the flour and cornflour over the surface and beat in with 2 tbsp hot water plus the vanilla extract. Gently fold in the whisked egg whites with a metal spoon. Do not over-mix, but make sure all the egg white is incorporated.

3 Spoon a heaped dessert spoon of the mixture into the cupcake cases, and bake for about 12 minutes, or until well risen, golden, and the centres spring back when lightly pressed. Transfer to a wire rack to cool.

4 Meanwhile, prepare the filling and topping. Select 6 small or 3 large strawberries cut into halves or quarters, including their green hulls, and reserve for decoration. Hull and chop the remainder and sweeten to taste with a little of the sugar, and sharpen with a few drops of lemon juice. Whip the cream and the remaining sugar until peaking.

5 Cut out a circle of sponge from each cake so you end up with a small well in the centre, leaving a 5mm ($^{1}/_{4}$in) border all round. Fill with the chopped strawberries. Pipe or spoon the whipped cream on top, and put a strawberry half, or quarter, on the top of each. Place the cut out rounds of sponge at a jaunty angle to the side of the strawberries and press gently into the cream to secure.

makes 12

**prep 15 mins
• cook 12 mins**

**12-cup
standard
bun tray
• standard
cupcake cases**

Blueberry and pistachio angel cupcakes

These look beautiful and taste sublime. Serve for tea or dessert.

INGREDIENTS
55g (2oz) shelled pistachio nuts
2 large egg whites
pinch of salt
$^1/_2$ tsp cream of tartar
115g (4oz) caster sugar
40g (1$^1/_4$oz) plain flour
20g ($^3/_4$oz) cornflour
$^1/_4$ tsp natural almond extract
$^1/_4$ tsp pure vanilla extract
85g (3oz) dried blueberries

For the cream cheese frosting
150ml (5fl oz) double cream
4 tbsp icing sugar
140g (5oz) cream cheese
a few fresh or extra dried blueberries (optional)

METHOD
1 Preheat the oven to 160°C (325°F/Gas 3). Line the bun tray with 12 cupcake cases.

2 Put the pistachios in a bowl, cover with boiling water and leave to stand for 5 minutes. Drain, then rub off the skins in a clean tea towel. Finely chop the nuts. Set aside half for decoration.

3 Place the egg whites in a clean, dry glass or metal bowl and lightly whisk until foamy. Whisk in the salt and cream of tartar, and continue to whisk until the egg whites stand in stiff peaks.

4 Sift the sugar, flour, and cornflour over the egg whites, add the almond and vanilla extracts, the dried blueberries, and half the chopped nuts, then fold in gently with a metal spoon until just combined.

5 Spoon the mixture into the cupcake cases, and bake for about 25 minutes, or until risen, pale biscuit-coloured, and just firm to the touch. Transfer to a wire rack to cool.

6 To make the frosting, place the cream in a bowl and lightly whip with the icing sugar. Then whisk in the cream cheese until softly peaking. Spoon the frosting on top of the angel cakes and decorate with the reserved pistachio nuts and a few fresh or dried blueberries, if using.

makes 12

prep 25 mins
• cook 25 mins

12-cup
standard
bun tray
• standard
cupcake cases

Cherry and coconut cupcakes

This classic combination of flavours is always popular. If you like, the cakes can be coloured pink as well as the icing.

INGREDIENTS

115g (4oz) glacé cherries, quartered
115g (4oz) butter, at room temperature
115g (4oz) caster sugar
2 eggs
85g (3oz) self-raising flour
55g (2oz) desiccated coconut, plus extra for dusting
1½ tsp baking powder
few drops of natural pink food colouring (optional)

For the icing

175g (6oz) butter, at room temperature
350g (12oz) icing sugar, sifted
4 tsp milk
few drops of natural pink food colouring
25g (scant 1oz) desiccated coconut
12 glacé cherries

METHOD

1 Preheat the oven to 180°C (350°F/Gas 4). Line a bun tray with 12–15 cupcake cases. Wash, dry, and quarter the cherries.

2 Put the butter, sugar, eggs, flour, coconut, and baking powder in a large mixing bowl and beat well with a wooden spoon or an electric hand whisk until light and fluffy. Add the quartered cherries. If using, add a few drops of pink food colouring and beat briefly again.

3 Spoon the mixture into the cupcake cases, and bake for about 15 minutes, or until well risen, golden, and the centres spring back when lightly pressed. Transfer to a wire rack to cool.

4 To make the icing, beat the softened butter in a bowl. Gradually beat in the icing sugar and milk until soft and fluffy. Beat in a few drops of pink food colouring. Pipe or spoon the icing on top of the cupcakes, and top each with a dusting of desiccated coconut and a glacé cherry.

makes 12–15

prep 15 mins
• cook 15 mins

**standard
bun tray
• standard
cupcake cases**

Coffee walnut cupcakes

A stylish cupcake for morning coffee or afternoon tea.

INGREDIENTS
- 85g (3oz) walnut halves, finely chopped
- 115g (4oz) butter, at room temperature
- 115g (4oz) caster sugar
- 115g (4oz) self-raising flour
- $\frac{1}{2}$ tsp baking powder
- 2 eggs
- 2 tsp instant coffee granules, dissolved in 2 tsp hot water

For the coffee icing
- 1 tbsp instant coffee granules, dissolved in 1 tbsp hot water
- 175g (6oz) butter, at room temperature
- 350g (12oz) icing sugar, sifted
- 12 walnut halves

METHOD

1 Preheat the oven to 180°C (350°F/Gas 4). Line a bun tray with 12–15 cupcake cases.

2 Place the butter, caster sugar, flour, baking powder, eggs, and the instant coffee solution in a large mixing bowl and beat well with an electric hand whisk or a wooden spoon until light and fluffy. Fold in the walnuts with a metal spoon.

3 Spoon the mixture into the cupcake cases, and bake for about 15 minutes, or until well risen, golden, and the centres spring back when lightly pressed. Transfer to a wire rack to cool.

4 Meanwhile, make the icing. Place the instant coffee solution in a bowl. Beat in the butter and gradually add the sifted icing sugar, beating until light and fluffy. Pipe or spoon the icing on top of the cooled cupcakes. Decorate each with a walnut half.

makes 12–15

**prep 15 mins
• cook 15 mins**

**standard
bun tray
• standard
cupcake cases**

Vanilla cheesecake

This rich yet light cheesecake is guaranteed to be a crowd pleaser.

INGREDIENTS

60g (2oz) unsalted butter
225g (8oz) digestive biscuits,
  finely crushed
1 tbsp demerara sugar
675g (1½lb) full-fat cream cheese,
  at room temperature
4 eggs, separated
200g (7oz) caster sugar
1 tsp pure vanilla extract
500ml (16fl oz) soured cream
kiwi fruit slices, to garnish

METHOD

1 Preheat the oven to 180°C (350°F/Gas 4). Lightly grease or line the base of the springform tin with baking parchment.

2 Melt the butter in a small saucepan over a medium heat. Add the biscuit crumbs and demerara sugar, and stir until blended. Press the crumbs over the base of the tin.

3 Combine the cream cheese, egg yolks, 150g (5½oz) of the caster sugar, and the vanilla in a bowl, and beat until blended. In a separate clean, dry glass or metal bowl, beat the egg whites until stiff. Fold the egg whites into the cream cheese mixture. Pour the mixture into the tin and smooth the top.

4 Place the tin in the oven and bake for 45 minutes, or until just set in the middle. Remove the tin from the oven and leave it to stand for 10 minutes, or until it sinks back into the tin.

5 Meanwhile, combine the soured cream and remaining sugar in a bowl, and beat until the sugar has dissolved. Pour on top of the cheesecake and smooth the surface. Increase the oven temperature to 240°C (475°F/Gas 9), return the cheesecake to the oven, and continue baking for a further 5 minutes. Leave to cool completely on a wire rack, then cover and chill for at least 6 hours. When ready to serve, garnish with slices of kiwi fruit.

serves 10–12

prep 20 mins,
plus standing
and chilling
• cook 50 mins

allow at least
6 hrs for
chilling

23cm (9in)
round
springform
cake tin

Strawberry cheesecake

This no-cook cheesecake is incredibly easy to make.

INGREDIENTS

50g (1³/₄oz) unsalted butter
100g (3¹/₂oz) dark chocolate, broken into pieces
150g (5¹/₂oz) digestive biscuits, finely crushed
400g (14oz) mascarpone
grated zest and juice of 2 limes
2–3 tbsp icing sugar, plus extra for dusting
225g (8oz) strawberries

METHOD

1 Melt the butter and chocolate in a small saucepan over a very gentle heat, and stir in the biscuit crumbs. Transfer the mixture to the flan tin, and press it down firmly and evenly into the tin.

2 Beat the mascarpone in a bowl with the lime zest and juice. Stir in the icing sugar, to taste. Spread the cheese mixture over the biscuit base, then cover and refrigerate for at least 1 hour.

3 To serve, hull and halve the strawberries and arrange them over the cheesecake. Dust with icing sugar and cut into slices.

PREPARE AHEAD The cheesecake can be made up to 24 hours in advance, and chilled until required.

serves 8–10

prep 15 mins,
plus chilling

20cm (8in)
round
loose-
bottomed
flan tin

Lemon poppy seed cheesecake with berry purée

A light alternative to a biscuit-based cheesecake, especially good for a lunchtime dessert.

INGREDIENTS

2 lemons
300g (10oz) cottage cheese
300g (10oz) cream cheese
250ml (9fl oz) soured cream
200g (7oz) caster sugar
3 tbsp cornflour
4 eggs
1½ tbsp poppy seeds
icing sugar, for dusting
strawberries and raspberries,
   to decorate

For the berry purée

250g (9oz) fresh, frozen, or preserved berries, such as
   blackberries, bilberries, raspberries, and strawberries
85g (3oz) caster sugar

METHOD

1 Preheat the oven to 150°C (300°F/Gas 2). Grease and line the cake tin with baking parchment. Grate the zest from the lemons and squeeze the juice. Place the cheeses, soured cream, sugar, cornflour, lemon zest, and ²/₃ of the lemon juice into a food processor, and process until smooth.

2 Add the eggs and process to combine. Stir in the poppy seeds, pour the mixture into the prepared tin (the mixture should fill ¹/₂–²/₃ of the tin), and bake for 1 hour 30 minutes, or until the cheesecake is firm.

3 Meanwhile, to make the berry purée, place the berries, sugar, and remaining lemon juice in a food processor and blend until smooth. Chill, covered, until needed.

4 When the cheesecake is cooked, remove from the oven and run a knife around the edge of the tin to loosen the cake, and to stop the surface cracking when cooling. Let it cool in the tin on a wire rack, then cover and chill for at least 5 hours. When ready to serve, remove from the tin, dust with icing sugar and serve with the fresh fruit and the berry purée.

serves 6–8

prep 20 mins
• cook 1 hr
30 mins

allow at least
5 hours
for chilling

23cm (9in)
round
springform
cake tin
• food
processor

freeze for
up to 3 months

Blueberry-ripple cheesecake

The tartness of the blueberry fruit purée is the perfect foil for the smooth richness of this baked cheesecake.

INGREDIENTS

125g (4^1/$_2$oz) digestive biscuits
50g (1^3/$_4$oz) unsalted butter
150g (5^1/$_2$oz) blueberries
150g (5^1/$_2$oz) caster sugar,
    plus 3 tbsp extra
400g (14oz) cream cheese
250g (9oz) mascarpone
2 large eggs, plus 1 large egg yolk
^{1}/$_2$ tsp pure vanilla extract
2 tbsp plain flour

METHOD

1 Preheat the oven to 180°C (350°F/Gas 4). Grease the cake tin. Put the biscuits in a large food bag and crush with a rolling pin. Melt the butter in a pan, then add the biscuit crumbs and stir until well-coated. Press the crumbs into the base of the tin.

2 Put the blueberries and the 3 tbsp of caster sugar in a food processor and whiz until smooth, then push the mixture through a nylon sieve into a small pan. Bring to the boil, then allow to simmer for 3–5 minutes, or until thickened and jammy. Set aside. Rinse the goblet of the food processor.

3 Put all the remaining ingredients into the food processor and whiz until well combined. Pour the mixture on to the biscuit base and smooth the top. With a teaspoon, carefully drizzle the blueberry mixture over the cream cheese mixture in a swirly pattern. Bake the cheesecake for 40 minutes, or until it has set but still has a slight wobble in the middle when you shake the tin. Leave to cool in the oven for an hour, then cool completely and serve.

serves 8

**prep 20 mins
• cook 40 mins**

**20cm (8in)
deep round
loose-
bottomed
cake tin
• food
processor**

Baked stem ginger cheesecake

Fragrant ginger gives this cheesecake a new dimension.

INGREDIENTS

200g (7oz) digestive biscuits
25g (scant 1oz) unsalted butter
4 eggs, at room temperature, separated
175g (6oz) golden caster sugar
150g tub cream cheese, at room temperature
250g tub mascarpone
2 tbsp syrup from a jar of stem ginger
4–5 balls stem ginger, sliced into fine strips
2 tbsp plain flour

METHOD

1 Preheat the oven to 180°C (350°F/Gas 4). Grease and line the base of the springform tin with baking parchment. Put the digestive biscuits in a plastic bag and crush with a rolling pin. Alternatively, whiz them in a food processor. Melt the butter in a pan, add the biscuits, then stir until well combined. Spoon into the tin and press firmly into the base.

2 Put the eggs yolks and sugar in a mixing bowl and whisk with a balloon whisk or an electric hand whisk until pale, thick, and creamy. Stir in the cream cheese and mascarpone, then beat with a wooden spoon until smooth. Add the ginger syrup and the sliced stem ginger and stir well. Sift in the flour and fold in with a metal spoon.

3 Put the egg whites in a clean, dry glass or metal bowl and whisk until stiff peaks form. Fold into the egg yolk mixture, then spoon over the biscuit base. Bake for 50 minutes, or until golden and almost set – the cheesecake should still wobble slightly. Turn the oven off and leave the cake in there to cool. Release from the tin and serve.

serves 6

**prep 30 mins
• cook 50 mins**

**20cm (8in)
round
springform
cake tin**

Black cherry cheesecake

This fresh cheesecake has a light texture and lemony taste, while the juicy cherries and syrup add a rich colour and sweet flavour.

INGREDIENTS

75g (2¹/₂oz) butter
200g (7oz) digestive biscuits, crushed
2 x 250g tubs ricotta cheese
75g (2¹/₂oz) golden caster sugar
zest and juice of 4 lemons
142ml carton double cream
11g sachet powdered gelatine
400g can black cherries or morello
  cherries in juice

METHOD

1 Grease and line the sprinform tin. Melt the butter in a pan, add the biscuits, and stir until well coated. Transfer the mixture to the tin, pressing it down firmly with the back of a spoon so that it is level.

2 Mix the ricotta cheese, sugar, and lemon zest together in a bowl. Put the cream in a bowl and whip lightly with a balloon whisk until it forms soft peaks. Add to the ricotta mixture, and beat with a wooden spoon until well combined.

3 Mix the lemon juice and gelatine in a small heatproof bowl, then sit the bowl over a pan of simmering water, and stir until the gelatine dissolves. Add to the ricotta mixture and stir well. Pour the mixture on top of the biscuits, spreading it out evenly. Cover and place in the refrigerator for a couple of hours or until set and firm.

4 Meanwhile, drain the cherries, pouring the juice into a pan. Bring the juice to the boil, then allow to simmer for 10 minutes, or until the juice has reduced by ³/₄. Leave to cool, then pile the cherries on top of the cheesecake, spoon over the sauce, and serve.

serves 6

prep 20 mins,
plus chilling
• cook 10 mins

allow at least
2 hrs for
chilling

20cm (8in)
round
springform
cake tin

White chocolate cheesecake

The decadent white chocolate filling is coated with crisp dark chocolate.

INGREDIENTS

150g (5$\frac{1}{2}$oz) digestive biscuits
50g (1$\frac{3}{4}$oz) unsalted butter
200g (7oz) white chocolate
500g (1lb 2oz) ricotta cheese
2 large eggs
100g (3$\frac{1}{2}$oz) dark chocolate, melted
4 tbsp double cream
fresh raspberries, to serve

METHOD

1 Preheat the oven to 160°C (325°F/Gas 3). Line the springform tin with baking parchment and grease the sides. Place the biscuits in a sturdy plastic bag, and crush with a rolling pin.

2 Melt the butter in a small saucepan and stir in the biscuit crumbs. Press evenly and firmly into the cake tin, smoothing over with the back of a wooden spoon. Chill in the refrigerator until needed.

3 Melt the white chocolate in a heatproof bowl set over a pan of barely simmering water, stirring occasionally. Beat the ricotta and eggs in another bowl until smooth, then mix in the melted white chocolate. Spoon the mixture on to the biscuit base. Put the springform tin on a baking sheet. Bake for 45 minutes until set. Remove from the oven and leave to cool in the tin.

4 When the cheesecake has cooled, release it from the tin and transfer to a serving plate. Melt the dark chocolate in a heatproof bowl set over a pan of barely simmering water, and stir in the cream. Spread the chocolate mixture evenly over the cheesecake. Cover and chill for 2–3 hours, or preferably overnight. Scatter over the fresh raspberries, and serve.

serves 6

prep 25 mins,
plus chilling
• cook 45 mins

allow 2–3 hrs
for chilling,
or overnight
if possible

20cm (8in)
springform
cake tin

Mini banana and chocolate cheesecakes

These no-cook mini cheesecakes look and taste fabulous. Irresistible!

INGREDIENTS

125g (4$\frac{1}{2}$oz) all-butter shortbread biscuits
25g (scant 1oz) unsalted butter
100g (3$\frac{1}{2}$oz) white chocolate,
   broken into pieces
200g (7oz) cream cheese
2 large eggs, separated
100ml (3$\frac{1}{2}$fl oz) double cream

15g ($\frac{1}{2}$oz) sachet gelatine
50g (1$\frac{3}{4}$oz) caster sugar
2 bananas, sliced
juice of $\frac{1}{2}$ lemon
50g (1$\frac{3}{4}$oz) dark chocolate, grated,
   to decorate

METHOD

1 Line the bun tray with 12 cupcake cases. Place the shortbread biscuits in a plastic bag and crush them with a rolling pin. Place the butter in a small saucepan over a gentle heat and stir until melted. Remove from the heat, add the biscuit crumbs, and mix well. Divide the mixture between the paper cases, pressing down firmly, then cover and chill in the refrigerator for about 30 minutes.

2 Place the chocolate in a small heatproof bowl, set it over a saucepan of simmering water, and stir occasionally until the chocolate has melted. Set aside.

3 Place the cream cheese, egg yolks, and cream in a large bowl, beat together until smooth, then stir in the melted chocolate. Set aside.

4 Place 3 tbsp of cold water in a small saucepan, sprinkle over the gelatine, and place over a gentle heat. Swirl the liquid around and stir constantly, making sure the water does not boil, until the gelatine is dissolved. Immediately remove the saucepan from the heat, and stir the gelatine suspension into the cheesecake mixture. Set aside.

5 Place the egg whites in a clean, dry glass or metal bowl and whisk until stiff peaks form. Continue whisking as you gradually incorporate the sugar. Add the whisked egg whites to the cheesecake mixture and fold in. Divide the mixture between the paper cases, cover, and refrigerate for at least 3 hours.

6 Once the cheesecakes are set, carefully remove them from the paper cases, loosening them first with a small knife. Finish by slicing the bananas and tossing them in the lemon juice to prevent them from browning. Make a circle of banana slices on top of each cheesecake, and sprinkle with grated chocolate.

PREPARE AHEAD The cheesecakes can be kept, covered, in the paper cases without topping for up to 1 day in the refrigerator.

makes 12

**prep 30 mins,
plus chilling
• cook 10 mins**

**allow at least
3 hrs
for chilling**

**standard
12-cup
bun tray
• standard
cupcake cases**

Lemon meringue roulade

The traditional roulade filling is given a new twist in this impressive dessert.

INGREDIENTS

5 egg whites
225g (8oz) caster sugar
$^{1}/_{2}$ tsp white wine vinegar
1 tsp cornflour
$^{1}/_{2}$ tsp pure vanilla extract
250ml (9fl oz) double cream
4 tbsp ready-made lemon curd
icing sugar, for dusting

METHOD

1 Preheat the oven to 180°C (350°F/Gas 4), and line the baking tin with baking parchment.

2 Place the eggs whites in a clean, dry glass or metal bowl and whisk until stiff peaks form. Continue whisking at a slower speed and gradually add the caster sugar, a little at a time. Gently fold in the vinegar, cornflour, and vanilla extract.

3 Spread the mixture into the tin, and bake in the centre of the oven for 15 minutes. Remove from the oven and allow to cool.

4 Meanwhile, whisk the cream until thick, and fold in the lemon curd until blended.

5 Turn the cooled roulade out on to another piece of baking parchment, and peel off the parchment it was cooked on. Spread the lemon cream evenly over the roulade. Roll the meringue and keep covered and chilled. Slice the roulade when ready to serve.

PREPARE AHEAD The meringue can be stored for up to 1 week in a dry, airtight tin.

serves 8

prep 30 mins
• cook 15 mins

25 × 35 cm
(10 × 14in)
shallow baking
tin or Swiss
roll tin

❄

freeze for
up to 2 months

Apricot meringue roulade

The delicate flavour of apricots is intensified by adding passion fruits, which have a wonderful perfume that makes this roulade rather special.

INGREDIENTS

4 large egg whites
salt
225g (8oz) caster sugar
25g (scant 1oz) flaked almonds
icing sugar, to dust
300ml (10fl oz) double cream
400g can apricot halves
   (240g drained weight)
seeds and pulp from 2 passion fruits

METHOD

1 Preheat the oven to 190°C (375°F/Gas 5). Line the Swiss roll tin with baking parchment. Place the egg whites in a clen, dry glass or metal bowl with a pinch of salt, and whisk until soft peaks form. Whisk in the sugar 1 tbsp at a time until the mixture is stiff and shiny. Spoon into the Swiss roll tin and smooth into the corners. Scatter the flaked almonds over the top, then bake for 15–20 minutes, or until just firm to the touch and golden. Turn the meringue out on to a sheet of baking parchment dusted with icing sugar, and leave to cool.

2 Meanwhile, place the cream in a chilled bowl and whisk until soft peaks form. Spread the cream over the meringue, then scatter over the apricots and passion fruit seeds. Roll the meringue up, starting from one short end and using the parchment to help you. Cover and keep chilled. When ready to serve, dust with a little more icing sugar.

serves 8

prep 30 mins
• cook 20 mins

32.5 x 23cm
(13 x 9in)
Swiss roll tin

freeze for
up to 2 months

Classic Pavlova

This classic meringue dessert is named after Russian ballerina Anna Pavlova, but credit for inventing it is claimed by both Australia and New Zealand.

INGREDIENTS

6 egg whites, at room temperature
pinch of salt
350g (12oz) caster sugar
2 tsp cornflour
1 tsp vinegar
300ml (10fl oz) double cream
strawberries, kiwi fruit, and passion fruit,
   to decorate

METHOD

1 Preheat the oven to 180°C (350°F/Gas 4). Line a baking tray with baking parchment. Put the egg whites in a large clean, dry glass or metal bowl with a pinch of salt. Whisk until stiff, then start whisking in the sugar 1 tbsp at a time, whisking well after each addition. Continue whisking until the egg whites are stiff and glossy, then whisk in the cornflour and vinegar.

2 Spoon the meringue on to the baking tray and spread to form a 20cm (8in) circle. Bake for 5 minutes, then reduce the oven heat to 140°C (275°F/Gas 1), and cook for a further 1 hour 15 minutes, or until the outside is crisp. Allow it to cool completely before transferring to a serving plate.

3 Whip the cream until it holds its shape, then spoon it on to the meringue base. Decorate with the fruit and serve.

PREPARE AHEAD You can make the meringue base up to a week in advance, and store it in a dry, airtight tin.

serves 6

prep 15 mins
• cook 1 hr
20 mins

Meringue and rum layer cake

Brown sugar goes well with rum, and makes the meringue quite chewy.

INGREDIENTS

85g (3oz) caster sugar
85g (3oz) dark soft muscovado sugar
3 egg whites

For the filling

250g (9oz) mascarpone
30g (1oz) caster sugar
115g (4oz) dark chocolate, chopped
150ml (5fl oz) double cream
3 tbsp rum
85g (3oz) toasted chopped hazelnuts
115g (4oz) pitted black cherries, drained weight
icing sugar, for dusting

METHOD

1 Preheat the oven to 130°C (250°F/Gas ¹/₂). Draw three 18cm (7in) diameter circles on a piece of baking parchment.

2 To make the meringue, mix the sugars together. In a clean, dry glass or metal bowl, whisk the egg whites until very stiff, and gradually whisk in the sugar. Divide among the 3 circles and spread flat. Bake for 1¹/₂ hours, or until crisp and dry. Transfer to a wire rack to cool.

3 To make the filling, beat the mascarpone and sugar together in a large bowl. Melt the chocolate in a heatproof bowl over a pan of simmering water. Allow to cool for 10 minutes.

4 Stir the chocolate into the mascarpone mixture. Whip the cream until it just holds its shape, then add to the mascarpone, along with the rum, nuts, and cherries.

5 Place a meringue circle on a serving plate, spread half the filling over the meringue, and place a second meringue on top. Spread the remaining chocolate mixture over the second meringue and place the last meringue on top. Chill for at least 30 minutes, then dust with icing sugar before serving.

serves 4–6

prep 30 mins, plus chilling • cook 1 hr 30 mins

Rhubarb and ginger meringue cake

The classic combination of rhubarb and ginger, makes a tasty filling for this delicious meringue cake.

INGREDIENTS
4 egg whites
pinch of salt
225g (8oz) caster sugar

For the filling
600g (1lb 5oz) rhubarb, chopped
85g (3oz) caster sugar
4 pieces of stem ginger, chopped
$^1/_2$ tsp ground ginger
250ml (9fl oz) double cream
icing sugar, to dust

METHOD
1 Preheat the oven to 180°C (350°F/Gas 4). Place baking parchment on 2 baking trays.

2 Whisk the egg whites, the pinch of salt, and 115g (4oz) sugar in a large clean, dry glass or metal bowl until stiff, glossy peaks form. Fold in the rest of the sugar, a spoonful at a time.

3 Divide the meringue between the baking trays and spread into 18cm (7in) circles. Bake for 5 minutes, then reduce the oven temperature to 130°C (250°F/Gas $^1/_2$), and bake for 1 hour. Open the oven door and leave the meringue to cool completely.

4 Meanwhile, put the rhubarb, caster sugar, chopped stem ginger, ground ginger, and water in a large saucepan and cook, covered over a low heat for 20 minutes, or until soft. Allow to cool. If too wet, drain to get rid of some of the liquid, and chill until required.

5 Whip the cream and fold in the rhubarb. Place 1 meringue on a serving plate, spread it with rhubarb and ginger filling, and top with the remaining meringue. Dust with icing sugar and serve.

PREPARE AHEAD Make the meringues up to 1 week in advance; store in an airtight container.

serves 6–8

**prep 30 mins,
plus cooling
• cook 1 hr**

Mountain meringue cake

The perfect chewy teatime or dessert cake, especially if you have a sweet tooth.

INGREDIENTS

4 large egg whites
225g (8oz) golden caster sugar
115g (4oz) ready-to-eat dried
  apricots, chopped
115g (4oz) pitted dates, chopped
2 tsp cocoa powder
1 tsp instant coffee granules, dissolved in
  1 tbsp boiling water
1 tsp cocoa powder, to decorate
1 tbsp sesame seeds, to decorate

For the nut buttercream

50g (1¾oz) 70 per cent dark chocolate
50g (1¾oz) unsalted butter, at
  room temperature
100g (3½oz) crunchy peanut butter
100g (3½oz) icing sugar

METHOD

1 Preheat the oven to 190°C (375°F/Gas 5). Lightly oil the cake tins and line the base of each with a circle of baking parchment.

2 Place the egg whites in a large clean, dry glass or metal bowl, and beat with a balloon whisk or an electric whisk until very stiff peaks form. Add the sugar, 1 tbsp at a time, beating until the mixture is very thick and glossy peaks form. Fold in the apricots, dates, cocoa powder, and coffee solution with a metal spoon.

3 Divide the mixture between the prepared cake tins and smooth level. Place in the lower third of the oven and bake for 40 minutes, or until the meringues are golden and crispy on top. Remove from the oven and allow to cool completely in the tins.

4 When you are ready to assemble the cake, make the nut buttercream. Place the chocolate in a small heatproof bowl, set it over a saucepan of simmering water, and stir occasionally until the chocolate has melted. Place the butter, peanut butter, icing sugar, and melted chocolate in a large bowl, and beat until the mixture is thick and well blended.

5 Remove the meringues from the tins, place one meringue on a plate, and spread with the nut buttercream. Sandwich together with the second meringue. Decorate by dusting with cocoa powder, then sprinkle with sesame seeds. Refrigerate for several hours before serving, to allow the nut buttercream to harden slightly. Remove from the refrigerator about an hour before serving to bring the cake to room temperature.

PREPARE AHEAD The meringues can be kept, unfilled, in an airtight container for 1 day, but are best eaten the day they are made.

GOOD WITH Fresh fruits, such as raspberries or pears.

serves 8–10

prep 30
mins, plus
assembling
and chilling
• cook 40 mins

allow several
hours for
chilling

two 20cm
(8in) round
cake tins

freeze the
meringues,
unfilled, for
up to 1 month

221

INDEX

Page numbers in *italics* indicate illustrations.

A
almonds
    Almond and orange cake 78, *79*
    Apple streusel cake *28*, 82, *83*
    Berry friands *26*, 154, *155*
    Cherry and almond cake 70, *71*
    Chocolate almond cake 60, *61*
    French almond financiers *25*, 148, *149*
    Orange and pistachio cake *27*, 74, *75*
    Panforte *132*, 133
    Raspberry cupcakes *176*, 177
    Raspberry, lemon, and almond bake 136, *137*
    Sticky lemon cake *27*, 68, *69*
    Stollen 110, 111
angel cakes
    Angel food cake 36, *37*
    Blueberry and pistachio angel cupcakes
        20, 184, *185*
    Tropical angel cake *21*, 84, *85*
apples
    Apple muffins *22*, 160, *161*
    Apple streusel cake *28*, 82, *83*
    Cinnamon apple and sultana cupcakes
        178, *179*
    Toffee apple traybake *28*, 138, *139*
apricots
    Apricot cake 66, *67*
    Apricot crumble shortbread *26*, 134, *135*
    Apricot meringue roulade *212*, 213
    Mountain meringue cake *29*, 220, 221

B
baking powder 6
baking soda 6
bananas
    Banana bread 96, *97*
    Banana and chocolate chip muffins *22*, *158*, 159
    Banana, cranberry, and walnut loaf
        26, 104, *105*
    Mini banana and chocolate cheesecakes
        23, 206, *207*
    Toffee-topped banana cake *20*, 90, *91*
Bee sting cake (Bienenstich) *20*, 44, *45*
beetroot, Superfood loaf cake *27*, 108, *109*
berries
    Berry friands *26*, 154, *155*
    Lemon poppy seed cheesecake with berry
        purée 196, *197*
    see also specific berries (eg raspberries)
bicarbonate of soda 6
Bienenstich *20*, 44, *45*
biscuit cake, Chocolate *22*, *24*, 142, *143*
Black Forest gâteau *20*, 92, *93*
blondies, White chocolate and macadamia nut
    22, 116, 117
blueberries
    Berry friands *26*, 154, *155*
    Blueberry muffins *24*, 162, *163*
    Blueberry and pistachio angel cupcakes
        20, 184, *185*
    Blueberry-ripple cheesecake *29*, 198, *199*
Brazil nuts, Toffee-topped banana cake
    20, 90, *91*
brownies
    Double chocolate 114, *115*
    Toffee 118, *119*
    White chocolate and macadamia nut blondies
        22, 116, 117
butter 6
buttercream
    Cherry and coconut cupcakes
        23, 186, *187*

Chocolate and buttercream Swiss roll
    23, 42, *43*
Chocolate-frosted cupcakes 170, *171*
Cinnamon apple and sultana cupcakes
    178, *179*
Coffee walnut cupcakes 188, *189*
Fondant fancies *22*, 152, *153*
Mountain meringue cake *29*, 220, 221
Orange and lemon cupcakes *20*, *22*, 172, *173*
Rich vanilla buttercream icing 18

C
cake tins, choosing and preparing 7, *13*
candied peel
    Florentine slices 130, *131*
    Panforte *132*, 133
    Stollen 110, *111*
carrots
    Almond and orange cake 78, *79*
    Carrot cake *24*, 76, *77*
cheesecakes
    Baked stem ginger *29*, 200, *201*
    basic recipe and technique *14*
    Black cherry *25*, *29*, *202*, 203
    Blueberry-ripple *29*, 198, *199*
    Lemon poppy seed, with berry
        purée 196, *197*
    Mini banana and chocolate *23*, 206, *207*
    Strawberry *25*, *194*, 195
    Vanilla 192, *193*
    White chocolate 204, *205*
cherries
    Black cherry cheesecake *25*, *29*, *202*, 203
    Black Forest gâteau *20*, 92, *93*
    Cherry and almond cake 70, *71*
    Cherry and coconut cupcakes
        23, 186, *187*
    Cherry flapjacks 128, *129*
    Meringue and rum layer cake *28*, 216, *217*
chocolate
    Banana and chocolate chip muffins
        22, *158*, 159
    Black Forest gâteau *20*, 92, *93*
    Cherry flapjacks 128, *129*
    Chocolate almond cake 60, *61*
    Chocolate Amaretti roulade *29*, 50, *51*
    Chocolate biscuit cake *22*, *24*, 142, *143*
    Chocolate and buttercream Swiss roll
        23, 42, *43*
    Chocolate cake with chocolate fudge icing
        20, 46, *47*
    Chocolate cupcakes 174, *175*
    Chocolate ganache 60, *61*
    Chocolate log *21*, 48, *49*
    Chocolate muffins *24*, 164, *165*
    Chocolate-frosted cupcakes *23*, 170, *171*
    Florentine slices 130, *131*
    Marble cake *26*, 54, 55
    Meringue and rum layer cake *28*, 216, *217*
    Mocha slice *28*, 126, *127*
    Mountain meringue cake *29*, 220, 221
    Pear and chocolate cake *28*, 88, 89
    preparation techniques *17*
    Sachertorte *21*, 52, *53*
    Sticky toffee shortbreads *22*, *124*, 125
    see also brownies; white chocolate
coconut
    Cherry and coconut cupcakes *23*, 186, *187*
    Coconut and lime cake *21*, 80, 81
    Florentine slices 130, *131*
    Tropical angel cake *21*, 84, *85*
coffee
    Coffee walnut cupcakes 188, *189*
    Mocha slice *28*, 126, *127*

Mountain meringue cake *29*, 220, 221
Nutty "drop" buns *24*, 150, 151
Pecan, coffee, and maple cake 56, *57*
cranberries, Banana, cranberry, and walnut loaf
    26, 104, *105*
cream, whipping and piping *16*
cream cheese
    icings and frostings 76, *77*, *80*, 81, 184, *185*
    see also cheesecakes
crème pâtissière 19
crumble shortbread, Apricot *26*, 134, *135*
cupcakes
    Blueberry and pistachio angel *20*, 184, *185*
    Cherry and coconut *23*, 186, *187*
    Chocolate 174, *175*
    Chocolate-frosted *23*, 170, *171*
    Cinnamon apple and sultana 178, *179*
    Coffee walnut 188, *189*
    Lime drizzle *27*, 180, 181
    Orange and lemon *20*, *22*, 172, *173*
    Raspberry *176*, 177
    Strawberry and cream *22*, 182, *183*
    Vanilla *21*, 168, 169
curls, chocolate *17*

D
dates
    Mountain meringue cake *29*, *220*, 221
    Nutty "drop" buns *24*, 150, 151
    Sticky date flapjacks *23*, 122, *123*
    Tropical fruit and ginger cake *26*, 72, 73
"drop" buns, Nutty *24*, 150, 151

E
eggs 6, *10–11*
equipment 7

F
figs, Panforte *132*, 133
financiers, French almond *25*, 148, *149*
Flapjacks 120, *121*
    Cherry 128, *129*
    Sticky date *23*, 122, *123*
flours 6
Fondant fancies *22*, 152, *153*
friands, Berry *26*, 154, *155*
fruit cakes
    Caribbean tea bread 102, *103*
    Celebration cake *21*, 86, *87*
    Florentine slices 130, *131*
    Light fruitcake *26*, 64, 65
    Stollen 110, *111*
    Superfood loaf cake *27*, 108, *109*
    Tropical fruit and ginger cake *26*, 72, 73
    see also specific fruits (eg lemons)

G
ganache, Chocolate 60, *61*
ginger
    Baked stem ginger cheesecake *29*, 200, *201*
    Marmalade and ginger loaf *27*, *106*, 107
    Rhubarb and ginger meringue cake *29*, 218, *219*
    Tropical fruit and ginger cake *26*, 72, 73
glacé icing 98, 99, 100, *101*, *150*, 151

H
hazelnuts
    Meringue and rum layer cake
        28, 216, *217*
    Panforte *132*, 133
honey
    Honey cake *29*, 58, *59*
    Honey loaf *98*, 99
    Panforte *132*, 133

I

icings and frostings
Angel food cake frosting 36, *37*
Celebration cake icing 86, *87*
chocolate fudge 20, *46*, 47
chocolate ganache 60, *61*
chocolate glaze 52, *53*
cream cheese 76, *77*, *80*, 81, 184, *185*
fondant 152, *153*
glacé 98, 99, 100, *101*, *150*, 151
honey 44, *45*, 98, 99
pecan, coffee, and maple 56, *57*
piping technique *16*
toffee 90, *91*
see also buttercream
ingredients 6

L

lemons
Black cherry cheesecake 25, 29, *202*, 203
Lemon, lime, and poppy seed cake 26, 100, *101*
Lemon meringue roulade 210, *211*
Lemon poppy seed cheesecake with berry purée 196, *197*
Lemon poppy seed muffins 24, 156, *157*
Orange and lemon cupcakes 20, 22, 172, *173*
Raspberry, lemon, and almond bake 136, *137*
Sticky lemon cake 27, 68, 69
limes
Coconut and lime cake 21, *80*, 81
Lemon, lime, and poppy seed cake 26, 100, *101*
Lime drizzle cupcakes 27, *180*, 181
lining cake tins *13*

M

macadamia nuts, White chocolate and macadamia nut blondies 22, *116*, 117
Madeira cake 32, *33*
Madeleines 22, 24, 146, *147*
mango
Caribbean tea bread 102, *103*
Tropical angel cake 21, 84, *85*
Tropical fruit and ginger cake 26, *72*, 73
Marble cake 26, 54, 55
Marmalade and ginger loaf 27, *106*, 107
mascarpone
Baked stem ginger cheesecake 29, *200*, *201*
Blueberry-ripple cheesecake 29, *198*, *199*
Meringue and rum layer cake 28, *216*, *217*
Strawberry cheesecake 25, *194*, 195
meringues
Apricot meringue roulade *212*, 213
Classic Pavlova 29, 214, *215*
Lemon meringue roulade 210, *211*
Meringue and rum layer cake 28, *216*, *217*
Mountain meringue cake 29, *220*, 221
Rhubarb and ginger meringue cake 29, 218, *219*
muffins
Apple 22, 160, *161*
Banana and chocolate chip 22, *158*, 159
Blueberry 24, 162, *163*
Chocolate 24, 164, *165*
Lemon poppy seed 24, 156, *157*

N

no-bake cakes
Black cherry cheesecake 25, 29, *202*, 203
Chocolate biscuit cake 22, 24, 142, *143*

Mini banana and chocolate cheesecakes 23, 206, *207*
Strawberry cheesecake 25, *194*, 195
nuts *see* specific types (eg almonds)

O

oats *see* flapjacks
oranges
Almond and orange cake 78, *79*
Orange and lemon cupcakes 20, 22, 172, *173*
Orange and pistachio cake 27, 74, *75*

P

Panforte *132*, 133
paper cases 7
passion fruit
Apricot meringue roulade *212*, 213
Classic Pavlova 29, 214, *215*
Tropical angel cake 21, 84, *85*
Pavlova, Classic 29, 214, *215*
peanut butter, Mountain meringue cake 29, *220*, 221
Pear and chocolate cake 28, 88, 89
pecan nuts
Apple muffins 22, 160, *161*
Pecan, coffee, and maple cake 56, *57*
Toffee brownies 118, *119*
pineapple
Caribbean tea bread 102, *103*
Tropical angel cake 21, 84, *85*
Tropical fruit and ginger cake 26, *72*, 73
piping technique *16*
pistachio nuts
Blueberry and pistachio angel cupcakes 20, 184, *185*
Orange and pistachio cake 27, 74, *75*
poppy seeds
Lemon, lime, and poppy seed cake 26, 100, *101*
Lemon poppy seed cheesecake with berry purée 196, *197*
Lemon poppy seed muffins 24, 156, *157*
prunes, Honey cake 29, 58, 59

R

raspberries
Berry friands 26, 154, *155*
Raspberry cupcakes *176*, 177
Raspberry, lemon, and almond bake 136, *137*
Rhubarb and ginger meringue cake 29, 218, *219*
ricotta cheese
Black cherry cheesecake 25, 29, 202, 203
White chocolate cheesecake 204, *205*
roulades and Swiss rolls
Apricot meringue roulade *212*, 213
Chocolate Amaretti roulade 29, 50, *51*
Chocolate and buttercream Swiss roll 23, 42, *43*
Chocolate log 21, 48, *49*
Lemon meringue roulade 210, *211*
rolling technique *15*
Swiss roll 24, 40, *41*

S

Sachertorte 21, 52, *53*
seeds
Superfood loaf cake 27, 108, *109*
see also poppy seeds
separating eggs *10*
shortbread
Apricot crumble shortbread 26, 134, *135*
Mocha slice 28, 126, *127*
Sticky toffee shortbreads 22, *124*, 125

sponge cakes
basic recipe and technique *12*
Bienenstich 20, 44, *45*
Chocolate almond cake 60, *61*
Chocolate cake with chocolate fudge icing 20, *46*, 47
Coconut and lime cake *21*, *80*, 81
Fondant fancies 22, 152, *153*
Honey cake 29, 58, *59*
Madeira cake 32, *33*
Madeleines 22, 24, 146, *147*
Marble cake 26, 54, 55
Pecan, coffee, and maple cake 56, *57*
Sachertorte 21, 52, *53*
Vanilla sponge 34, *35*
Victoria sponge cake 27, 38, 39
White chocolate cakes 28, *140*, 141
see also angel cakes; cupcakes; roulades and Swiss rolls
Stollen 110, *111*
strawberries
Classic Pavlova 29, 214, *215*
Strawberry cheesecake 25, *194*, 195
Strawberry and cream cupcakes 22, 182, *183*
streusel cake, Apple 28, 82, *83*
sugars 6
Swiss rolls *see* roulades and Swiss rolls

T

tea
Caribbean tea bread 102, *103*
Honey cake 29, 58, *59*
techniques *10–17*
tins, choosing and preparing 7, *13*
toffee
Sticky toffee shortbreads 22, *124*, 125
Toffee apple traybake 28, *138*, *139*
Toffee brownies 118, *119*
Toffee-topped banana cake 20, 90, *91*

V

vanilla
Rich vanilla buttercream icing 18
Vanilla cheesecake 192, *193*
Vanilla cupcakes 21, *168*, 169
Vanilla sponge 34, *35*
Victoria sponge cake 27, 38, 39

W

walnuts
Banana bread 96, *97*
Banana, cranberry, and walnut loaf 26, 104, *105*
Coffee walnut cupcakes 188, *189*
Nutty "drop" buns 24, *150*, 151
White chocolate cakes 28, *140*, 141
whipping cream *16*
whisking egg whites *11*
white chocolate
Mini banana and chocolate cheesecakes 23, 206, *207*
Raspberry cupcakes *176*, 177
Sticky toffee shortbreads 22, *124*, 125
White chocolate cakes 28, *140*, 141
White chocolate cheesecake 204, *205*
White chocolate and macadamia nut blondies 22, *116*, 117

Y

yeast-raised cakes
Bienenstich 20, 44, *45*
Stollen 110, *111*

ACKNOWLEDGMENTS

DORLING KINDERSLEY WOULD LIKE TO THANK THE FOLLOWING:

Photography
Carole Tuff, Tony Cambio, William Shaw, Stuart West, David Munns, David Murray, Adrian Heapy, Nigel Gibson, Kieran Watson, Roddy Paine, Gavin Sawyer, Ian O'Leary, Steve Baxter, Martin Brigdale, Francesco Guillamet, Jeff Kauck, William Reavell, Jon Whitaker

Indexer
Susan Bosanko

And the following for work on additional recipes
Carolyn Humphries for the cupcake recipes; Yvonne Allison, Ah Har Ashley, Anna Guest, Mrs J Hough, Tracy McCue, Juliet Montefiore, Catherine Parker, Jean Piercy, Emma Shibli, Penelope Tilston, Janet Wilson, and Galina Varese for recipe writing; Hilary Mandleberg for recipe editing; Jane Milton and the recipe testers at Not Just Food; William Reavell for photography; Jane Lawrie for food styling; Sue Rowlands for prop styling.

Useful information

Oven temperature equivalents

CELSIUS	FAHRENHEIT	GAS	DESCRIPTION
110°C	225°F	$1/4$	Cool
130°C	250°F	$1/2$	Cool
140°C	275°F	1	Very low
150°C	300°F	2	Very low
160°C	325°F	3	Low
180°C	350°F	4	Moderate
190°C	375°F	5	Moderately hot
200°C	400°F	6	Hot
220°C	425°F	7	Hot
230°C	450°F	8	Very hot
240°C	475°F	9	Very hot

Volume equivalents

METRIC	IMPERIAL	METRIC	IMPERIAL
30ml	1fl oz	450ml	15fl oz
60ml	2fl oz	500ml	16fl oz
75ml	$2^1/2$fl oz	600ml	1 pint
100ml	$3^1/2$fl oz	750ml	$1^1/4$ pints
120ml	4fl oz	900ml	$1^1/2$ pints
150ml	5fl oz ($1/4$ pint)	1 litre	$1^3/4$ pints
175ml	6fl oz	1.2 litres	2 pints
200ml	7fl oz ($1/3$ pint)	1.4 litres	$2^1/2$ pints
240ml	8fl oz	1.5 litres	$2^3/4$ pints
300ml	10fl oz ($1/2$ pint)	1.7 litres	3 pints
350ml	12fl oz	2 litres	$3^1/2$ pints
400ml	14fl oz	3 litres	$5^1/4$ pints